ENCYCLOPEDIA
OF
SEWING MACHINE
TECHNIQUES

ENCYCLOPEDIA
OF
SEWING MACHINE
TECHNIQUES

NANCY BEDNAR

JOANN PUGH-GANNON

Sterling Publishing Co., Inc.,
New York

A Sterling/Sewing Information Resources Book

Sewing Information Resources

Owner: JoAnn Pugh-Gannon
Photography: Kaz Ayukawa, K Graphics
Book Design and Electronic Page Layout: Ernie Shelton, Shelton Design Studios
Index: Mary Helen Schiltz

Library of Congress Cataloging-in-Publication Data Available

A Sterling/Sewing Information Resources Book

10 9 8 7 6 5 4 3 2 1

Published by Sterling Publishing Company, Inc.
387 Park Avenue South, New York, N.Y. 10016
Produced by Sewing Information Resources
P.O. Box 330, Wasco, Il. 60183
©1999 by Nancy Bednar & JoAnn Pugh-Gannon
Distributed in Canada by Sterling Publishing
c/o Canadian Manda Group, One Atlantic Avenue, Suite 105
Toronto, Ontario, Canada, N6K 3E7
Distributed in Great Britain and Europe by Cassell PLC
Wellington House, 125 Strand, London WC2R 0BB, England
Distributed in Australia by Capricorn Link (Australia) Pty Ltd.
P.O. Box 6651, Baulkham Hills, Business Centre, NSW 2153,
Printed in the United States
All rights reserved.

Sterling ISBN 0-8069-6393-X

FOREWORD

Having spent many years of my sewing career working for an international sewing machine manufacturer, I have experienced the pleasure of learning many things my sewing machine will do for me. As with any tool or piece of equipment, no matter the field of interest, the more you understand how to use it, the more you will benefit from the knowledge.

It was always my dream to produce a book full of sewing machine techniques so you, the sewer, could benefit from this knowledge. You would learn more about the many presser feet that are available and the novelty threads, needles, and fabrics there are to use to complete these techniques. It is up to you to try them all and have fun in the process!

Writing a book, like most projects—business or pleasure—has stops and starts. This book was no different! Unfortunately, one of the stops was not planned and quite tragic. It is to Nancy's late husband, Ed, that this book is dedicated.

But...now at its completion, I can justifiably say, "Hurrah! A job well done!"

DEDICATION

This book is dedicated to the memory of my husband, Ed, who sadly and unexpectedly passed away during the writing of this book. His patience in hearing the non-stop drone of sewing machines overhead at all hours of the day and night, and his constant support of my writing endeavors made squeezing 30 hours into a 24-hour day possible. His constant good humor in tolerating living with thousands of yards of fabric, countless spools of thread, and carry-out food cannot be replaced.

Thank you, Ed.

TABLE OF CONTENTS

INTRODUCTION

When sitting down to compose these beginning words, I wondered where to begin. As a sewing professional, I constantly hear that there are fewer and fewer people who are sewing. Why write a book for a smaller and smaller audience?

What we are hearing is wrong! Throughout my travels as a sewing teacher, I've spoken to group after group of enthusiastic, creative people who are every bit as passionate about working with their sewing machine, thread, and needle as I am. This book is written for them.

Like many young girls, began my sewing career progressively, dressing dolls, myself, every member of my family, my house, and even strangers, as a "sewing machine for hire." I've sampled sewing in many areas — from running a home-based bridal and home decorating business, teaching adults and children in private classes, and writing for national sewing publications, to ultimately authoring my first book, *Silk Ribbon Machine Embroidery*. Currently, as a consultant for an international sewing machine manufacturer, I enjoy product testing, project development, and teaching both retailers and consumers on a national level. Spending increasingly longer hours behind my sewing machine(s!) has not diminished my love of this creative craft one bit. If anything, it has encouraged me to explore and learn more and more myself. As I teach across the country, I'm encouraged to find so many,

many people who feel the same way.

This book is written for the seasoned sewer, as well as, the beginner, both of whom want to share their joy of creating. Fewer and fewer schools now include sewing in their curriculum due to budget cuts. In some areas of the country, it is difficult to even find beginning sewing classes. This book has been written as a reference guide to fill the knowledge gap, explaining classic as well as updated sewing techniques.

There is not a sewing technique that is too hard to learn. Each technique in this book has been written in an easy-to-follow manner with clear instructions and many step-by-step photos. Sample these techniques and then search for any one of the numerous books or articles written specifically about one of them, expanding your knowledge and experience in one area. Before long, you'll be a sewing expert yourself, adept at the many wonderful tricks and manipulations of fiber, thread, and machine.

Like most of you, I no longer sew out of necessity to save money or fill my closet with new garments for every day. Sewing is my passion and my joy. How lucky we are, as sewers, to see a picture in a magazine and confidently say, "I can make that!" It is my hope that this book will help you along that creative process, allowing you to bask in the glow of your talent.

Happy Creating!
Nancy Bednar

ETTING THE MOST FROM YOUR SEWING

Your sewing machine and all its accessories can provide you with hours of creativity and enjoyment. Most sewing machine manufacturers provide numerous extra accessories in addition to those standard with the machine. Often these "extra" feet become some of your most valuable. Take the time to learn the most you can about each — your machine and its feet!

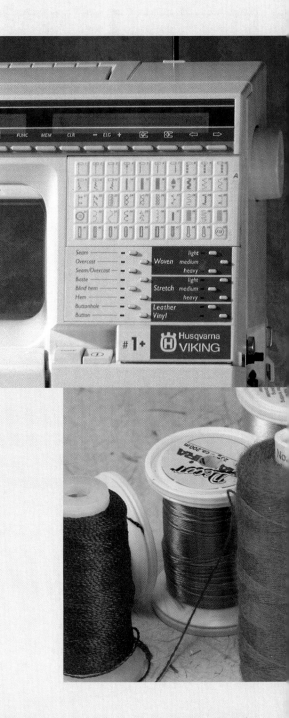

YOUR SEWING MACHINE

Your sewing machine is capable of endless creative possibilities far greater than straight stitching. This book is designed to teach you to use your machine as a practical and artistic tool and enable you to get greater enjoyment from the sewing machine you own.

A good place to start is to get to know your machine intimately. Even a machine with the most advanced technology won't help you sew better if you are not comfortable with it. Take time to get to know, or refresh yourself, with your machine's basic features and characteristics. Learn to recognize a "perfect stitch" and fundamentals, such as stitch length and width settings, reverse stitching, needle positions, and pressure and tension adjustments, which all affect stitch quality. Test out the different stitches on fabric scraps. Read and study the owner's manual cover-to-cover. If your machine manual is missing, contact a sewing machine dealer or the machine manufacturer for a new one. Be sure to know your machine's model number; it is often stamped on the bottom, on the back of a free-arm machine, or the front of a flatbed model. Once you are familiar with the fundamentals, they will become second nature and a part of your everyday sewing.

Beyond the basics, most machines come with a selection of standard presser, feet including a zig zag foot, buttonhole, blindhem, edgestitch, quilting guide, and more. Getting to know what

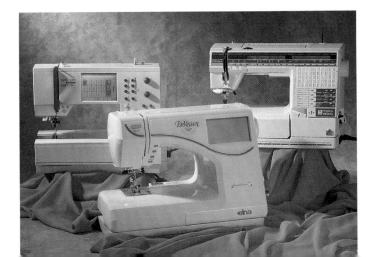

each one does will extend your machine's potential and give you more professional sewing results. Most presser feet can perform multi-purpose tasks, as you will see throughout this book.

Additional accessories and attachments are also available. Cording feet, pintucking feet, ruffler and fagoting attachments, for example, are just some of the many special accessories that will make even the most basic sewing machine models more useful. Check with your local sewing machine dealer for information on available attachments for your machine model. To locate a dealer in your area, check the Yellow Pages or contact the machine manufacturer/distributor of the brand you have. A resource list of

machine manufacturers is located in the back of this book.

A full-service sewing machine dealer will also stock new products that will aid your sewing. Specialized sewing machine needles, specialty threads, ribbons, and fabric stabilizers are just some of the new products available to the sewing market. A knowledgeable dealer will also offer in-store assistance on their uses.

A reputable sewing machine dealer can supply you with a wealth of knowledge. Many dealers offer a variety of classes from refreshers to advanced techniques. When purchasing a new machine be sure to sign up for the basic introductory lesson. Ask about supplementary workbooks, which may include fabric swatches and specific how-to's for your model. Many companies are producing basic videos for their new machines and accessories. They actually bring to life the owner's manual. You also may want to inquire about an 800 number for consumer call-ins.

Some sewing machine dealers sponsor sewing workshops taught by educational consultants from specific sewing machine manufacturers. Others may organize monthly sewing club meetings on particular topics and often invite sewing experts to give demonstrations on new techniques. Be sure to ask about a dealer's mailing list and add your name to it.

Other educational items a dealer may stock or have access to are instructional videos, how-to books, magazines, and pamphlets. Many of these items are produced by the sewing machine manufactures and offer tips and techniques on machine stitching and presser feet, as well as new product information.

Another valuable source of information is the Internet. The Internet has made available to the home-sewer a plethora of sewing information.

Sewing experts are now conducting on-line chat sessions. Many, if not all, of the sewing machine manufacturers and sewing products companies have Web sites to update the sewer with the latest sewing products. Sewing events may also be posted via the Internet. Sewing conferences and creative workshops offered in cities throughout the country are often promoted on-line. These expositions and conventions can be sponsored by sewing manufacturers or the American Sewing Guild (ASG) and are open to the general public. They are often called "sewer's heaven." They provide excellent opportunities to see first-hand the latest sewing techniques, shop for the newest products, and network with fellow sewers.

The American Sewing Guild is a national non-profit organization of home-sewers with local chapters across the country. The goal of the ASG is to provide up-to-date information and activities as well as monthly newsletters. It is a great way to learn and share information with enthusiastic stitchers right in your hometown. Local retailers generally work closely with these groups providing space in their shops for meetings, offering special discounts to members, and contributing expert advice. To see if a chapter of the ASG is in your area, contact the Home Sewing Association (address and Web site is listed in the back of this book under Important Information.). Or, ask about starting up a chapter yourself.

Care and Maintenance

Next to learning how to use your machine stitches and accessories, cleaning your machine is all-important. Keep the area under the feed dogs and the bobbin area clean. Oil your machine according to your owner's manual or check with your dealer. Every eight to twelve hours of sewing time or once a month should be sufficient. This will keep your machine running smooth and quiet and extend its life.

Some sewing machine companies suggest having your machine routinely serviced. This will depend on how frequently you sew and how diligent you are about keeping it cleaned and oiled. Computer machines tend to be more sensitive to lint than mechanical models and may need to be serviced more often.

Work Area and Lighting

Another aspect of sewing enjoyment and stress-free sewing is the workspace. Having a comfortable and safe place to sew is as important as the equipment you use. Your workplace doesn't need to be fancy or elaborate, but it does need to be functional. All you need to get going is a cleared-off surface for your machine and good lighting.

Studies have shown that the height of your work surface is an important consideration to ensure good posture and avoid strains, limit fatigue, and minimize energy expenditure. The industry standard for the height of your sewing machine work surface is 30 inches (from bed of machine to floor.) Use this standard when selecting your sewing surface. Furniture especially made for your sewing machine is designed for optimum comfort. The cutout area for the machine, for example, is positioned to the right to allow the sewer a better sewing position.

A chair is another important component to sewing comfort since sitting in one position for long periods of time can interfere with blood circulation and result in pain and numbness in the lower extremities. A well-designed chair helps maintain good posture, does not interfere with circulation, and equalizes the amount of pressure on the spine. Look at a seat depth of about 16 inches. Seat height should be adjustable from a seated position and a swivel is also helpful. The back of the chair should be contoured to support the inward curve of the back.

Start by correct placement of your light source. Ideally, the light source should come from behind you from one side. This way, the light is reflected away from the machine without casting a shadow. Incandescent lighting is most common in homes, but it is not the best for sewing. Fluorescent lights offer a line of light and minimize glare.

The color of the work surface and surrounding walls also contribute to your ability to see comfortably. The best choice for your sewing room walls is a flat white which reflects any light that strikes them.

In addition to your work surface and lighting, having a convenient and organized place to store your notions will help you use your machine better. Having accessories in a convenient sewing box, wicker basket, or in a rolling cart will make them handy when ready to use. If your sewing area is permanent, hang threads and notions, most often used, on a pegboard above your sewing machine.

Whether you are a new sewer, an experienced sewer, or one that is a little out of practice, we encourage you to use this book as your step-by-step guide to getting more satisfaction and fun from using your sewing machine.

NEEDLE AND THREAD OPTIONS

Needles

Your sewing machine is the most important piece of sewing equipment you own. But, sewing machine needles are almost as important as the machine itself. Perfect stitching requires the correct size and needle type. A dull, bent, or burred needle not only affects stitch quality, but your machine could be damaged. One good practice to follow is to insert a new needle in your machine before stitching a new project. Always change a needle after hitting a pin.

Use a good-quality needle of a brand recommended by your sewing machine dealer. It is a good idea to have a variety of machine needle sizes on hand so you will always have the right needle for the task. Most needles are interchangeable from machine to machine, but older models may require a special type. Check in your owner's manual or with your dealer for the correct type for your machine.

Needles are available in these types:

general-purpose or universal — produce good results on most fabrics and are available in sizes #60/8 to #110/18;

sharp points or stretch — needed for knits and stretch fabrics;

jeans — a sharp point to penetrate closely woven fabrics and available in size #90/14;

embroidery — designed with a thin shaft and sharp point to prevent the thread from fraying;

twin/triple — one shank and two or three fixed needles on a crossbar;

leather — wedge point for leather and vinyl; and.

hemstitching — specialty needle   with flanged sides. It is available in size #100/16 to #120/20.

When purchasing needles, you will find needle sizes are labeled with two numbers. The first number is the size given in metric measurement while the number following the slash is the American equivalent. The lower the number, the finer the needle. The higher number is a larger needle. Use the smallest needle possible for your fabric and thread. A too-large needle will cause puckering.

Thread

For the best-quality stitch, look for good-quality thread. Keep away from the bargain-brand threads. They will be made up of nubs with uneven thickness or fuzzy ends.

Thread selection will depend on your fabric type, type of stitching, and some personal preference. Most common thread types include cotton, polyester, cotton-wrapped polyester, rayon, metallic, and silk. Sewing thread also comes in three weights: extra fine, all-purpose, and top-stitching or buttonhole twist. For most straight stitching, a long-staple polyester or cotton-wrapped polyester is best. Try to match the thread, fabric weight, and the needle size. It is generally a good idea to use the same thread type in the bobbin and the needle for a perfect tension. This will not apply when using specialty and topstitching threads.

It is important to note that thread density is measured by its weight. The higher the thread-weight number, the thinner the thread. A 40-weight thread, for example, is thinner and lighter than a 30-weight. For decorative stitching with a filled-in look, select a thread with a lower weight number or use a thicker thread.

Decorative Threads

The list of special threads available for the sewing machine is growing. Rayon is a popular choice for decorative stitching because of it sheen. It is available in a variety of rich colors and in a variety of weights. Metallic threads are also readily available for the sewing machine.

The newer metallics are stronger than in the past and cause fewer machine glitches. Silk is another option for enhancing machine embroidery. Ribbon thread can now be purchased on spools. It is lightweight and can be used in the bobbin for decorative effects as well as for couching.

If your sewing machine dealer or fabric store has a limited selection of specialty threads, most can be mail-ordered. Check the Internet for selections.

Some threads will work better for certain techniques. It's always good to test the thread in your machine and on your fabric to determine which thread type will give the desired result you want. You will need to adjust the needle and bobbin tensions on your machine when using most of these specialty threads.

Here's a handy checklist to use when working with your machine:

♦ Read your machine manual carefully and understand your machine's functions, accessories, and attachments.

♦ Keep your manual handy as a quick reference.

♦ Keep your machine clean and lint free. Cover it when not in use.

♦ Use the correct presser foot for best results.

♦ Check for correct machine threading.

♦ Use a new sharp needle and be sure it is not bent.

♦ Match your needle with your thread.

♦ Insert the needle into the machine so that it is all the way up with the flat side to the back. (Check your manual first.)

♦ When using an embroidery hoop, keep the fabric taut.

♦ Don't pull or push the fabric while stitching. Let your machine do the work.

And, of course, use your sewing machine dealer as a resource. They are in business to help you get the most from your sewing!

CREATIVE TECHNIQUES

Adding unique or decorative treatments to your next garment or home decorating project can take it from the mundane to the sublime. More than 70 exciting, creative techniques are illustrated here in step-by-step form to inspire and excite you. Develop a time-saving, useful scrapbook as you experiment with each technique.

APPLIQUÉ, BASIC SATIN STITCH

Appliqué is defined as sewing a cutout decoration to a larger piece of fabric. Closely spaced zig zag stitches are sewn along the edge of the cut piece, both holding the fabric in place and providing a decorative, finished edge. Before the introduction of fusible webs, appliqué pieces were pinned or hand-basted to the larger fabric prior to satin stitching. Luckily, today's sewers can take advantage of these heat-activated products to make shifting and puckering a challenge of the past.

MACHINE SET-UP

- **Stitch:** Zig zag, L — ½, W — 2–2 ½, or scaled to an appropriate size for the appliqué piece
- **Presser Foot:** Open or clear embroidery foot
- **Needles:** Embroidery needle, size #75 or #90 Metafil needles for all metallic threads
- **Threads:** Needle — Rayon and cotton embroidery threads; metallic threads, either core-wound or film products
  Bobbin — All–purpose polyester or 60 wt. cotton embroidery
- **Tension:** Slightly loosened neddle at least one number
- **Optional:** Engage needle down function

FABRIC CHOICES:

Just about any fabric can be used for appliqué. Choose from loosely to firmly woven cottons, knits, silks, satins, metallics, and even, swimwear.

ADDITIONAL SUPPLIES:

- Pencil
- Paper-backed fusible webs, all weights
- Tear-away stabilizer

1 Appliqué design ideas can be found in many places, such as coloring books, wallpaper florals, greeting cards, or giftwrap. For best results, select an uncomplicated design.

2 Using a pencil, trace the design onto the paper side of the fusible web remembering that the design will be reversed when fused. For specific directional designs, numbers, and letters, flip the design on a photocopier prior to tracing. Cut out the design, leaving a ½" border all around.

3 Following the manufacturer's directions, iron the fusible web to the wrong side of your pre-washed fabric. Allow the fused design to cool completely, then cut it out and remove the backing paper. Fuse the appliqué in place, right side up.

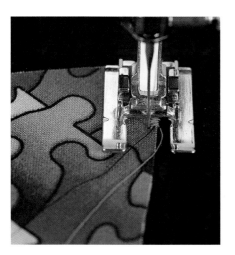

4 Set your machine for satin stitching following directions in Machine Set-Up. Layer the fabric over the tear-away stabilizer. Position the presser foot so that the center of the foot is slightly to the left of the outer edge of the fused appliqué piece. Turn the handwheel to sew one stitch. Gently pull on the needle thread

to coax the bobbin thread to the top of your work. Hold both threads in the center of the foot so they'll be caught in the tunnel of the zig zag stitch. Sew over the thread tails three to four times. Clip the threads.

continued

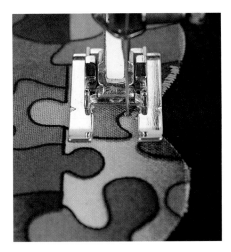 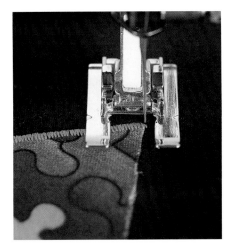

5 For inside corners, sew to the inside corner and into the shape by three to four zig zag stitches with the needle resting on the inside edge of the satin stitching. Lower your needle into the fabric and pivot. Reposition the foot along the edge of the fabric and continue to sew.

6 When stitching outside corners, sew past the corner by one zig zag stitch. Stop with the needle swing in the outside edge of the satin stitching. Lower your needle into the fabric and pivot. Reposition the foot and continue to sew.

7 Carefully remove all the stabilizer. Pull on the bobbin threads to expose a loop of needle thread. Pull the needle thread tail to the wrong side. Knot the threads together and clip.

Tips For appliqués with rounded edges, pivot around the curves frequently to create smooth, even outer edges. Always stop with your needle lowered into your work on the outer edge of the satin stitching. It is not unusual to stitch only three or four zig zag stitches before needing to pivot.

Determine an order of sewing when working with multi-layered designs. Decide which should be the most prominent point of your design and stitch it last. This will create a smooth and even row of stitching around this focal point in your design. For example, on a flower, satin-stitch around the

leaves first, then the outer petals, finishing with the center part of the flower.

APPLIQUÉ, BIAS BAR

Colorful bands of fabric, invisibly stitched in overlapping and undulating patterns, characterize this classic technique. Also called rouleau work, designs are often borrowed from ancient Celtic motifs. The clean-finished narrow tubes of fabric can be made quickly with the use of bias bar pressing strips. Then replace the painstaking hand-stitching process with built-in blindhem or pin stitching patterns to complete your design. Traditional rouleau work may have also included filler stitches similar to those used in Battenburg lace techniques.

MACHINE SET-UP

- **Stitch:** Blindhem or pin stitch, L — 2, W — 2
- **Presser Foot:** Edgestitch or clear embroidery foot
- **Needles:** Universal needle size #80 or matched to the base fabric
- **Threads:** Needle — Monofilament
  Bobbin — All-purpose polyester, color matched to the base fabric
- **Tension:** Normal
- **Optional:** Adjust needle position as necessary; engage needle down function; and reduce motor speed

FABRIC CHOICES:

Bias bars — Lightweight, all-natural fabrics that hold a crease
Base fabric — Medium weight, tightly woven fabrics

ADDITIONAL SUPPLIES:

- Heat-resistant plastic or metal press bars available in multi-size sets
- Chalk or fabric marker

26

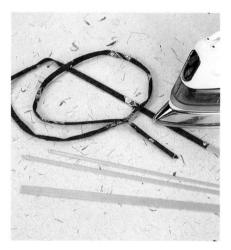

1 Follow the manufacturer's directions to cut, sew, and press the bias strips into appliqué bands.

2 Using a fabric marking tool, trace your desired appliqué design onto the base fabric.

3 Carefully pin the pressed bias strips onto the base fabric following the traced design. The stretch of the bias will allow the strips to mold easily around curves. Be careful to begin and end the strips underneath a previously pinned section to hide raw edges.

continued

4 Place your pinned design underneath the edgestitch or appliqué foot, positioning the folded edge of the fabric against the blade or toe on the foot. (Note: Stitch the inside curves first, followed by the outer curves. A quick press with an iron before beginning on the outer curves will coax the strip into stretching, creating a smoother outer curve.)

5 Begin to sew at a slow, even speed. The straight part of the stitch should fall just outside the folded edge of the bias strip. The horizontal part of your stitch should bite into the fabric tube, attaching it to the base fabric. Press the entire design when the stitching is complete.

Tip For an elegant look, create your bias strips from fine silks. The fabric is fluid and easily molds to the curving designs. Add filler stitches between the bands using your sewing machine or stitch by hand.

APPLIQUÉ, BLANKET STITCH

This charming folk-art edging technique can be traditionally found as the main stitch used to create "penny rugs". Coins were traced and cut from scrap wool, layered and bound with this decorative stitch sewn in heavy black thread. Sets of coin appliqués were then arranged side by side and whipstitched into a piece large enough for the desired project. Modern sewers can easily duplicate the stitched charm of yesteryear by using built-in stitches and heavier threads.

MACHINE SET-UP

- ◆ **Stitch:** Blanket or pin stitch, L and W — 2½–3
- ◆ **Presser Foot:** Open or clear embroidery foot
- ◆ **Needles:** Topstitch needle, size #90 or #100
- ◆ **Threads:** Needle — Topstitch thread or two strands of all-purpose polyester
  Bobbin — All-purpose polyester
- ◆ **Tension:** Normal
- ◆ **Optional:** Engage needle down function

FABRIC CHOICES:

Select wool or felt for traditional looks, solid cottons and historical prints for vintage looks. Retro prints from the '30s and '40s are also charming with blanket stitching.

ADDITIONAL SUPPLIES:

- ◆ Pencil
- ◆ Lightweight, fine fuse or traditional weight interfacing
- ◆ Tear-away stabilizer

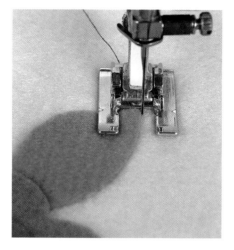 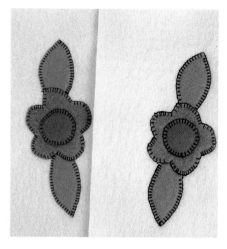

1 Following the directions in "Appliqué, Basic Satin Stitch," trace and fuse your desired design into place. Thread your needle with one or two threads. Select your stitch and adjust the length and width. Place a layer of tear-away stabilizer underneath the base fabric.

2 Position your presser foot so that the first vertical stitch sews exactly along the cut edge of the appliqué piece.

3 Continue to sew around the appliqué, sewing the horizontal part of the stitch onto the fused appliqué and the horizontal stitches just outside the cut edge. (Note: For better control, reduce

continued

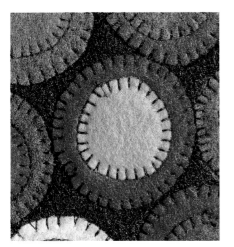

Tips If your sewing machine does not have a built-in pin or blanket stitch, try this adaptation. Select the honeycomb stitch with a L and W — 2½–3.

Or: Engage the Long Stitch function on your sewing machine. This function tells the machine to sew only every other stitch, manipulating the honeycomb pattern into a pin stitch on some machines.

your sewing machine motor speed while you become accustomed to how your selected stitch is formed. This will help in pivoting around corners with a continual, even stitch pattern.)

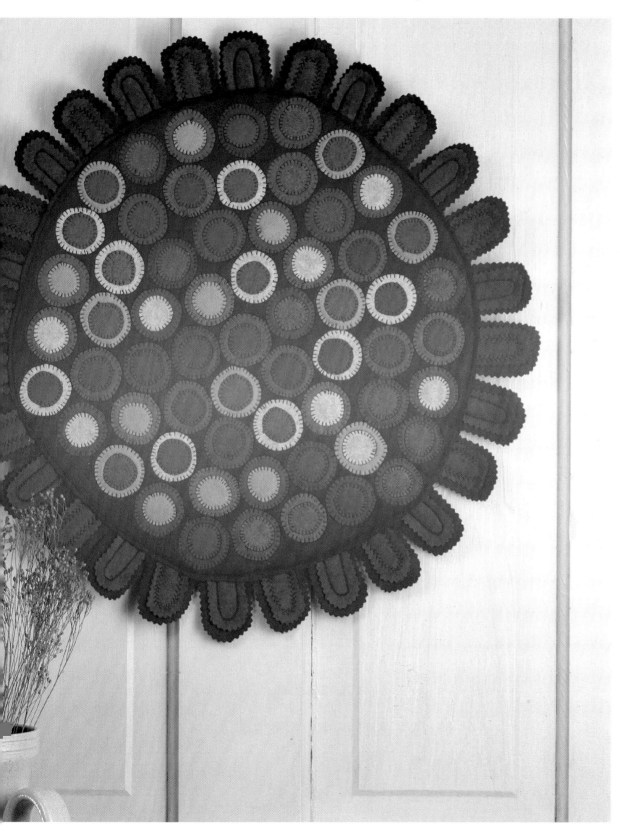

APPLIQUÉ, DECORATIVE STITCH

Explore your machine's decorative and utility stitch capabilities when sewing your next appliqué project. Forsake the usual satin-stitched edge for one or many of the options shown below.

MACHINE SET-UP

- **Stitch:** Utility, L and W — 2½–3
  Decorative, Preset L and W
- **Presser Foot:** Open or clear embroidery foot
- **Needles:** Embroidery needle, size #75 or #90
  Metafil or Metallica needles for metallic threads
- **Threads:** Needle — Rayon or cotton embroidery;
  metallics, either core-wrapped or polyester film products
  Bobbin — 60 wt. cotton embroidery
- **Tension:** Slightly loosened needle on decorative stitches, normal on utility stitches
- **Optional:** Engage needle down function

FABRIC CHOICES:

Same as "Appliqué, Basic Satin Stitch"

ADDITIONAL SUPPLIES:

- Pencil
- Fusible web
- Tear-away stabilizer

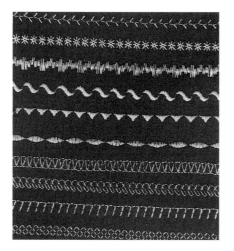

1 Refer to "Appliqué, Basic Satin Stitch" for cutting and fusing directions. Select a decorative or utility stitch pattern, adjusting the length and width according to Machine Set-Up recommendations. Place a layer of tear-away stabilizer underneath the base fabric.

2 Stitch around the appliqué shape. Complete the sewing and remove the stabilizer. Draw the needle thread to the wrong side, knot and clip the threaded tails.

Tips Certain stitches may require specific presser foot positioning. For the honeycomb stitch, center the foot over the fused appliqué edge. When using a stretch overlock stitch, position the vertical stitch along the cut edge and the angled stitch onto the appliqué. Place the vertical stitch of the jersey stitch at the cut edge and the angled stitch onto the appliqué. And, for the double overlock stitch, center the middle of the stitch over the appliqué edge.

APPLIQUÉ, FRAYED-EDGE

Frayed-edge appliqué is a fun and different method of appliqué. Your creativity knows no bounds using this technique. Printed or solid fabrics work equally well as the appliqués — the only criteria is the final result you desire. Cut, stitch, fold, and fray to your heart's content!

MACHINE SET-UP

- ♦ **Stitch:** Straight, L — 2–2½
- ♦ **Presser Foot:** Edgestitch, ¼", open embroidery, or all-purpose foot
- ♦ **Needles:** Match to fabric
- ♦ **Threads:** Needle and bobbin — All-purpose polyester
- ♦ **Tension:** Normal
- ♦ **Optional:** Engage needle down function

FABRIC CHOICES:

As desired for both base and appliqué fabrics

ADDITIONAL SUPPLIES:

- ♦ Rotary cutter and mat

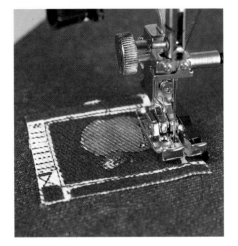 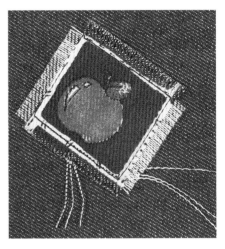

1 Determine the shape of the appliqué pieces you desire. Squares, rectangles, triangles, or even circles will work. Cut these shapes from your print or solid fabric of choice.

2 Pin your appliqué pieces on your base fabric in the design desired. If you are overlapping pieces, complete all the steps on the bottom piece before applying the top piece. Using your foot of choice, stitch the appliqué piece ¼" from the cut edge. Repeat stitching a second time.

3 Pull the threads along each edge up to the stitching lines. Complete your project according to the instructions.

continued

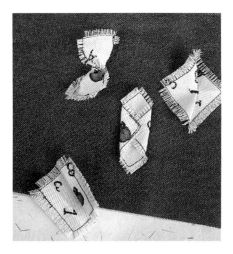

4 Frayed-edge appliqué pieces can also add a three-dimensional effect to your garment. Rather than stitching the appliqué piece directly to the base fabric, first stitch around the appliqué piece itself. Fray the edges, then fold the edges into the center, pleat the center, or twist the ends. Tack the appliqué pieces down in the center or as desired leaving the ends free.

Tip Be creative and design your own textured fabric using this frayed-edge appliqué technique.

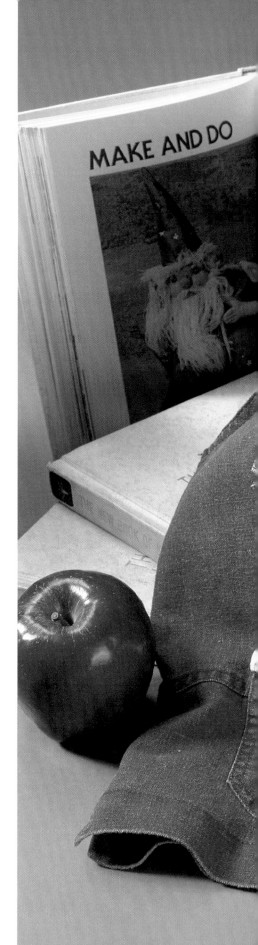

38

APPLIQUÉ, MADEIRA

Madeira work is a vintage, elegant technique first developed on the island of Madeira off the coast of Morocco. Traditionally, Madeira work is a combination of delicate embroidery stitches and fabrics. Today, it can be found accenting collars and cuffs, jacket edges, or hems. Most striking when sewn with two high contrast tones of fabric, our updated version relies on modern stabilizers and wing needle stitching to easily translate the process for the home sewer.

MACHINE SET-UP

- **Stitch:** Step One: Straight, L — ½
  Step Two: Pin stitch, L — 1½–2, W — 2½
- **Presser Foot:** Step One: All-purpose foot
  Step Two: Edgestitch or open embroidery foot
- **Needles:** Step One: Universal needle, size #70 or #80
  Step Two: Single wing needle, size #100–120
- **Threads:** Step One: Needle and bobbin — 60 wt. cotton embroidery
  Step Two: Needle — 60 wt. cotton or rayon embroidery
  Bobbin — 60 wt. cotton embroidery
- **Tension:** Normal to slightly tightened
- **Optional:** Engage needle down function

FABRIC CHOICES:

100% natural fibers are best, such as, light- to medium-weight linens, batiste, or fine broadcloth

ADDITIONAL SUPPLIES:

- Air- or water-soluble fabric marker
- Spray starch
- Appliqué or embroidery scissors
- Water-soluble, iron-on, and tear-away stabilizers

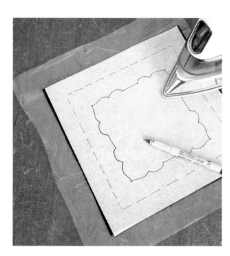

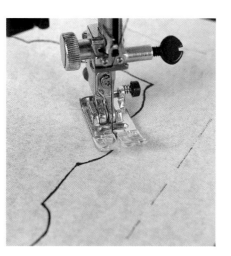

1 Mist the fabric with spray starch and iron dry. Using a permanent pen, trace both the appliqué design lines (solid line) and the outer stitching lines (broken line) onto a single layer of iron-on stabilizer. Fuse the stabilizer to the wrong side of your chosen border fabric. Layer the stabilized piece over a same-sized piece of water-soluble stabilizer. Pin all the layers together.

2 Using a short stitch length, sew on the outside stitching line through all the layers. Sew along the inner appliqué lines, using a thread color matched to the appliqué fabric.

3 Carefully, remove the iron-on stabilizer leaving a border piece of fabric with the water-soluble stabilizer sewn to it.

4 Layer the water-soluble stabilizer side against the right side of the base fabric. Stitch ¼" outside the outer stitching line through all the layers. Trim along outer edges, through all the layers, to a ⅛" seam, clipping and trimming the corners.

5 Trim the border fabric and water-soluble stabilizer to within ⅛" along the inner appliqué line, being careful not to cut through to the base fabric. Clip all curves and corners.

continued

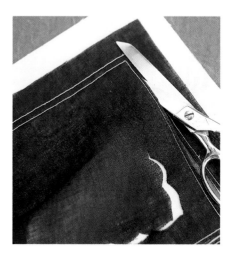

6 Turn the border fabric to the right side. Fold the water-soluble stabilizer to the inside, turning the edge under along the inner appliqué stitching line. The stabilizer will act as a facing making clean, crisp edges. (Note: A point turner will help turn crisp points.)

7 Reset the sewing machine for pin stitching in Step Two of Machine Set-Up. Remember to change your needle. Place a layer of tear-away stabilizer underneath the border and base fabric. Using the blade of the edgestitch foot as a guide, stitch the border in place.

8 Place your stitches so the vertical part of the stitch falls just outside the border edge, and the horizontal part of the stitch sews onto the border fabric. Remove the tear-away stabilizer.

APPLIQUÉ, MOLA

This traditionally colorful appliqué technique finds its roots with the Cuna Indians of the San Blas Islands in Panama. Primitive designs from nature, such as fish, flowers or small animals, are traditionally stitched into place using multiple layers of brightly colored fabrics. Edges are tediously hand–rolled and sewn down. A typical Mola can take up to a month to sew. This handwork process can be adapted for today's stitcher using the sewing machine and fusible products. An abundance of Mola design books exist providing authentic patterns for inspiration.

MACHINE SET-UP

- **Stitch:** Pin or blanket stitch
- **Presser Foot:** Open or clear embroidery foot
- **Needles:** Universal needle, size #80
- **Threads:** Needle — Cotton or rayon embroidery
  Bobbin — All-purpose thread, color matched to fabric
- **Tension:** Normal to slightly tightened needle

FABRIC CHOICES:

100% cotton in brightly colored solids or bold prints

ADDITIONAL SUPPLIES:

- Fusible web
- Fine–point permanent fabric marker
- Sharp embroidery scissors

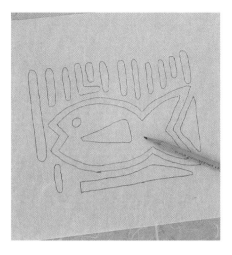

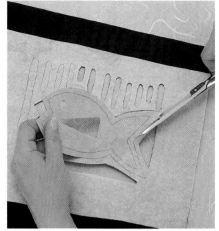

1 Trace the Mola design onto the paper side of the fusible web.

2 Place the web side of the fusible product to the wrong side of the top fabric. (Note: This fabric is called the design layer. Keep this fabric dark in color to avoid color bleed through with the underlay pieces.) Fuse in place.

3 Using sharp, embroidery scissors, cut out the design windows following the traced pattern.

4 Place a layer of brightly colored fabric underneath the design layer, so it shows through the cutout windows creating a foundation layer. Fill in the window

cutouts with different scraps of brightly colored fabrics underneath as inlays. Also place cutouts on top of the design layer as overlays.

5 When the design is complete, fuse all the layers together into one unit.

continued

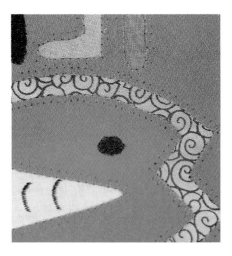

6 Adjust the sewing machine for the pin or blanket stitch following the directions above. Stitch around all the cutout windows to secure all layers. (Note: Position your stitches so the vertical portion of the stitch falls just beyond the cut edge and the horizontal stitch sews on the design layer.)

Tips Save the scrap–cutouts for future Mola–style embellishments. Most pin or blanket stitching will be done on the design layer, sewing along the edges of the cutout windows. Further enhance your Mola design using built–in decorative stitches. Look for simple, primitive–looking satin-stitch patterns, such as arrows, undulating waves or circles. Eyelet stitches make great bubbles!

APPLIQUÉ, NET

Appliqué using cotton nettingt is a wonderful technique that lends itself to heirloom garments and decorating items for the house. A layer of netting and organdy is all that is necessary for this wonderful sheer technique. Change a simple satin stitch by adding a cord for a raised effect giving dimension to the elegant design.

MACHINE SET-UP

- **Stitch:** Step One: Straight
  Step Two: Zig zag, L — ¾, W — 2
  Step Three: Zig zag, L — ½, W — 2½
- **Presser Foot:** Open embroidery foot, cording foot
- **Needles:** Universal needle, size #60–#70
- **Threads:** Needle and bobbin — 60 wt. cotton embroidery, color of choice
  Filler — Gimp or topstitching
- **Tension:** Slightly loosened needle
- **Optional:** Engage needle down function

FABRIC CHOICES:

Cotton netting and organdy
Batiste or lightweight linen as background fabric

ADDITIONAL SUPPLIES:

- Air- or water-soluble fabric marker
- Water-soluble stabilizer
- Gimp or topstitching thread
- Spring-loaded or wooden embroidery hoop
- Sharp-tipped embroidery or appliqué scissors

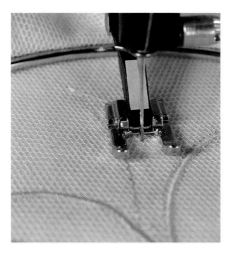

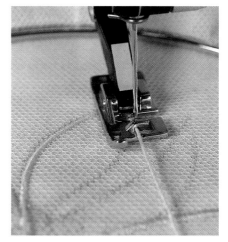

1 Transfer your design to one layer of water-soluble stabilizer. Layer the fabrics and stabilizer in the following order (from the bottom, right side up): water-soluble stabilizer with traced design, batiste, organdy, netting, and water-soluble stabilizer. Pin the layers together to avoid slipping. Place all the layers together into the spring hoop.

2 Set up your machine as outlined for Step One and stitch, following the design lines seen through the layers of sheer fabric and netting.

3 Using the Step Two settings, fill the cording foot with cord. Beginning in the center of the design, carefully begin stitching over the cord following the previous lines of stitching. Turn corners carefully making sure the cord remains in the satin stitching.

continued

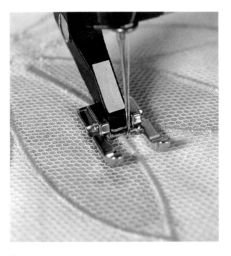

4 Carefully trim the water-soluble stabilizer and the batiste from the back of the design close to the line of stitches. Be careful not to pierce or clip the remaining organdy, netting, and water-soluble stabilizer.

5 Setting your machine using Step Three, satin-stitch again over-sewing the corded satin stitching.

APPLIQUÉ, REVERSE

There are many ways to appliqué. The best way for you to determine the technique to use is to test your base fabric. Some fabrics demand that the design be transferred directly to the stabilizer while others can handle having the design transferred to the appliqué fabric itself. Reverse appliqué is a method of first, transferring the design to the back of the base fabric, stitching from the back, trimming, and then satin-stitching from the front. This appliqué technique is particularly good for intricatly layered designs allowing for precise trimming and a more exact satin stitching along the edges.

MACHINE SET-UP

- **Stitch:** Step On: Straight
  Step Two: Satin Stitch, L — 1/2, W — 2–3
- **Presser Foot:** Open embroidery
- **Needles:** Universal needle, size #80
- **Threads:** Needle — Cotton or rayon embroidery
  Bobbin — 60 wt. cotton embroidery
- **Tension:** Slightly loosened needle
- **Optional:** Engage needle down function

FABRIC CHOICES:

Firm fabrics, such as twill, denim, or heavier cottons for base fabric
Cottons for appliqués

ADDITIONAL SUPPLIES:

- Air- or water-soluble fabric marker
- Fusible knit interfacing
- Firm tear-away stabilizer
- Appliqué scissors
- Plastic template material
- Optional: Spray adhesive

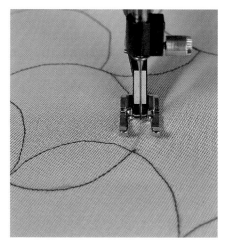

1 Fuse knit interfacing to the back of the base fabric. Cut your design from the plastic template material. Transfer the design to the back of the base fabric. (Note: Use a spray adhesive to hold the plastic template in place while tracing the design. The adhesive disappears within a few hours.)

2 With right sides up, layer the appliqué fabric over the base fabric making sure to cover the design area. Pin in place. Place a firm tear-away stabilizer over the appliqué fabric if necessary.

3 From the wrong side, straight-stitch around the design following the drawn guidelines.

continued

4 From the right side, trim away the excess fabric from around the appliqué using your appliqué scissors. Trim as close to the stitching line as possible without cutting any threads.

5 Set your machine for Step Two, selecting a satin-stitch width appropriate to the size of the design. From the right side, stitch around the design following and covering the straight stitching.

Tip For layered or more intricate appliqué designs, begin by straight stitching one layer at a time starting with the bottom layer. Once all the steps are completed on each layer, start on the next.

APPLIQUÉ, SHADOW

Shadow appliqué is a lovely, fine embellishment used pre-dominately with light-colored fabrics. Actually a variation of reverse appliqué, the appliquéd pieces are placed behind the base fabric and, when trimmed, the color "shadows" through. It is important to choose your fabrics carefully making sure you can see the appliqué fabric through the base fabric. A pin stitch or corded satin stitch outlines the design.

MACHINE SET-UP

♦ **Stitch:** Pin or narrow blanket stitch, L — 1–1½, W — 1–1½; satin stitch for corded appliqué
♦ **Presser Foot:** Open embroidery foot
♦ **Needles:** Universal needle, size #70
♦ **Threads:** Needle — Rayon or cotton embroidery
     Bobbin — 60 wt. cotton embroidery
♦ **Tension:** Normal
♦ **Optional:** Engage needle down function

FABRIC CHOICES:

Fine cotton batiste or linen in light colors
Stronger colored cotton or linen for appliqué

ADDITIONAL SUPPLIES:

♦ Air- or water-soluble fabric marker
♦ Spring-loaded or wooden embroidery hoop
♦ Appliqué scissors
♦ Optional: Lightweight tear-away stabilizer
     Gimp or topstitching thread for corded satin stitch

1 Trace the appliqué design onto the base fabric. Mark any section to be trimmed away with an X.

2 Layer the darker appliqué fabric under the base fabric and insert as one layer into your spring hoop.

3 Select a pin stitch and adjust the width and length proportionate to the design. From the top, begin stitching around the design, pivoting at the corners. Mirror image the design, if necessary, making sure the straight stitch portion of the pin stitch follows the outline and the zig zag stitch falls into the area of fabric that won't be cut away.

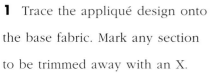

4 Remove the design from the hoop. Trim away all areas of the appliqué fabric from the back leaving the "shadow" design.

continued

5 As an option to the pin stitch, use a corded satin stitch to outline your design. Prepare your fabrics as in Steps 1 and 2. Follow the instructions for "Appliqué, Reverse," except straight-stitch from the top rather than the back following the traced design.

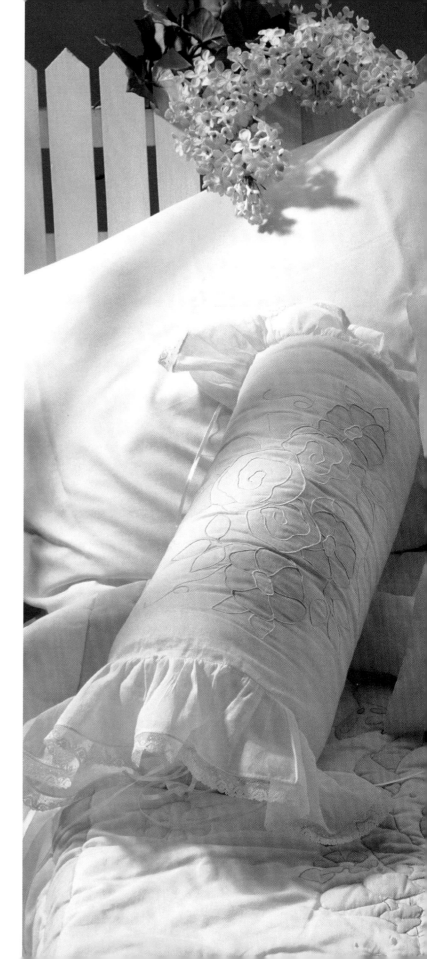

BATTENBURG, CONTEMPORARY LACEMAKING

Over a hundred years old, battenburg lacemaking is a technique that translates easily to contemporary use. The battenburg tape is formed into designs creating the base for a variety of filler stitches connecting the strips of tape. The filler stitches can easily be stitched free-motion on your sewing machine. For a beginner, a simple battenburg appliqué can add a nice touch to any garment.

MACHINE SET-UP

- ◆ **Stitch:** Straight
- ◆ **Presser Foot:** Darning or free-motion foot
- ◆ **Needles:** Universal needle, size #70 or #80
- ◆ **Threads:** Needle and bobbin — Cotton or rayon embroidery
- ◆ **Tension:** Normal to slightly loosened needle
- ◆ **Feed Dogs:** Lowered
- ◆ **Optional:** Engage needle down function

FABRIC CHOICES:

Battenburg tape

ADDITIONAL SUPPLIES:

- ◆ Water-soluble stabilizer
- ◆ Water-soluble fabric marker
- ◆ Spring-loaded or wooden embroidery hoop
- ◆ Pins

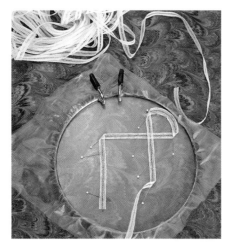

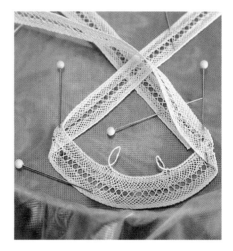

1 Transfer your design to the water-soluble stabilizer. Place the stabilizer in the hoop centering the design.

2 Begin pinning the battenburg tape to the stabilizer following the design. Leave a small amount of tape at the beginning to turn under.

3 At any curve, pull the header thread to gently mold the tape into shape. You may need to pull the thread in more than one location to form an even curve. Once the design is completed, fold back one end covering the raw end of the other.

continued

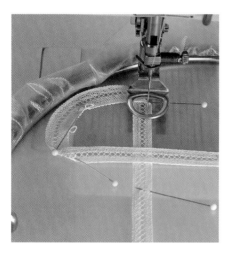 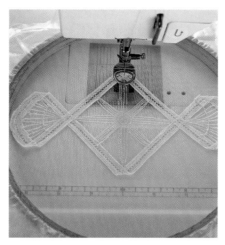

4 Remembering to lower your feed dogs, baste the tape in place along the inner and outer edges.

5 Moving the hoop yourself, begin designing filler stitches in the open areas connecting the tapes edges. Move across the stabilizer at an even pace creating the first bars. Add a spider web in the center to secure the bars.

6 Remove the piece from the hoop and carefully wash away the stabilizer. Press the battenburg lace piece into shape.

Tip Quality battenburg tape is reversible so flipping the tape at corners is okay.

If it is necessary to use multiple pieces of tape in one design, pin and baste each piece individually.

BOBBINWORK

Bobbinwork techniques allow the sewer to create with heavy or bulky threads and ribbons that are too large to pass through the eye of a sewing machine needle. Instead, these materials are wound onto a bobbin and placed into a loosened tension bobbin case. Stitches are sewn from the wrong side, using free-motion or built-in stitch patterns.

FABRIC CHOICES:

Firmly woven, medium-weight cottons, twills, or woolens. A medium- to heavyweight denim is ideal for a first bobbinwork project.

ADDITIONAL SUPPLIES:

- Secondary bobbin case with the ability to loosen tension
- Tear–away stabilizer
- Felt for padded bobbinwork appliqués

MACHINE SET-UP

Free-Motion Bobbinwork
- **Stitch:** Straight
- **Presser Foot:** Darning foot
- **Needles:** Universal needle, size #80 or #90
- **Threads:** Needle — All-purpose thread, color-matched to bobbin
  Bobbin — Pearl Crown Rayon, Ribbon Floss™, perle cotton, 2mm or 4mm silk ribbon, or smooth feeding, heavier threads
- **Tension:** Normal to slightly tightened needle
- **Feed Dogs:** Lowered

Decorative Stitch Bobbinwork
- **Stitch:** Any open, airy, pre-progammed stitch
- **Presser Foot:** Open embroidery foot or foot recommended for stitch chosen
- **Needles:** Universal needle, size #80 or 90
- **Threads:** Needle — All-purpose polyester, color-matched to bobbin
  Bobbin — Pearl Crown Rayon, Ribbon Floss™, Perle Cotton, 2mm or 4mm silk ribbon, smooth feeding, heavier thread
- **Tension:** Normal to slightly tightened needle
- **Feed Dogs:** Raised

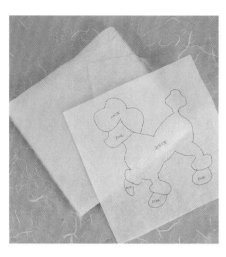

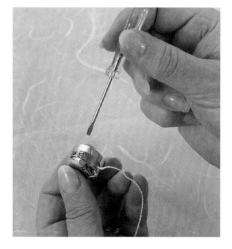

1 For free-motion padded designs, trace the design onto the paper side of fusible web. Fuse the web to the felt. Cut out the shape.

2 Fuse the felt shape to the right side of the garment. Straight-stitch the felt shape close to the edge providing an outline for the bobbin stitches.

3 Set the machine according to the information in Machine Set-Up. Wind a bobbin with a heavier thread of choice. (Note: Hand-wind ribbons or Ribbon Floss.) Insert the bobbin into a loose–tension secondary bobbin case adjusted so the bobbin thread pulls out easily.

continued

 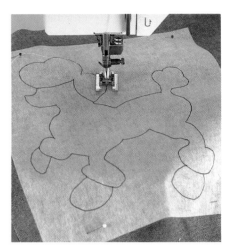

4 From the wrong side and following the traced design or stitched line, begin to sew small circles along markings. Overlap the stitches, varying the shape and length for texture and interest. Cover the design area completely. Draw the thread tails to the wrong side, tie, and clip.

5 For decorative stitch bobbinwork, set the machine according to the chart. Always test the selected stitches on a scrap of fabric using the chosen threads. Following the traced design or bobbin stitching, stitch the patterns at an even speed for best design formation. Draw the tails to the wrong side, tie and clip.

6 For unpadded or pre-programmed decorative stitch designs, trace the design onto a piece of tear-away stabilizer. Pin the stabilizer to the wrong side of the fabric. Stitch through the stabilizer using the traced lines as your guide.

Tips When most stitchers begin free-motion sewing, they often forget one thing—to breathe! Loose, straightened shoulders and regular breathing guarantees perfect stitch quality.

When beginning bobbinwork stitching, take one stitch bringing the heavier bobbin thread to the top. Lock both threads in place by sewing back and forth two or three times. Clip the thread tails.

CHARTED NEEDLEWORK

A unique embroidery technique, charted needle-work is actually closely aligned rows of raised satin stitching forming a design. Simple and quick to stitch, this technique can be used on any type of garment or home decorating project. Color changes are easy, too!

MACHINE SET-UP

- **Stitch:** Satin, L — ½, W — approximately 2–3
- **Presser Foot:** Piping or foot with deep groove on bottom
- **Needles:** Match to fabric
- **Threads:** Needle — Cotton or rayon embroidery
  Bobbin — 60 wt. cotton embroidery
- **Tension:** Slightly loosened needle
- **Optional:** Engage needle down function

FABRIC CHOICES:

As desired

ADDITIONAL SUPPLIES:

- Light- to medium weight tear-away stabilizer
- ¼" graph paper
- Various colors of marking pens
- Very small diameter knitting needle

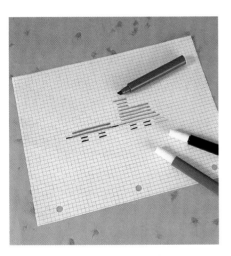

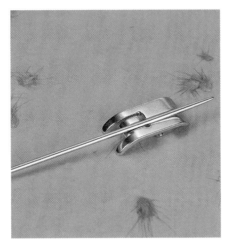

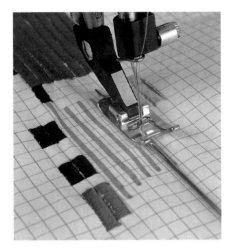

1 Using the colored marking pens, chart out the design on the graph paper changing colors of ink as you would change threads in the design.

2 Select a knitting needle approximately the same size as the groove on the bottom of the piping foot.

3 Layer the graph paper over the fabric with the tear-away stabilizer underneath. Pin all the layers together. Begin stitching over the colored lines with the zig zag stitches carefully floating over the knitting needle.

continued

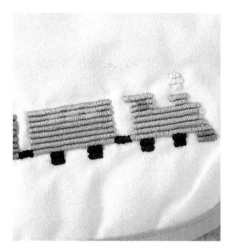

4 Change your thread colors as necessary following the design. Keep the rows of stitching close together with no space between.

5 Remove the stabilizer and graph paper once all the stitching is completed.

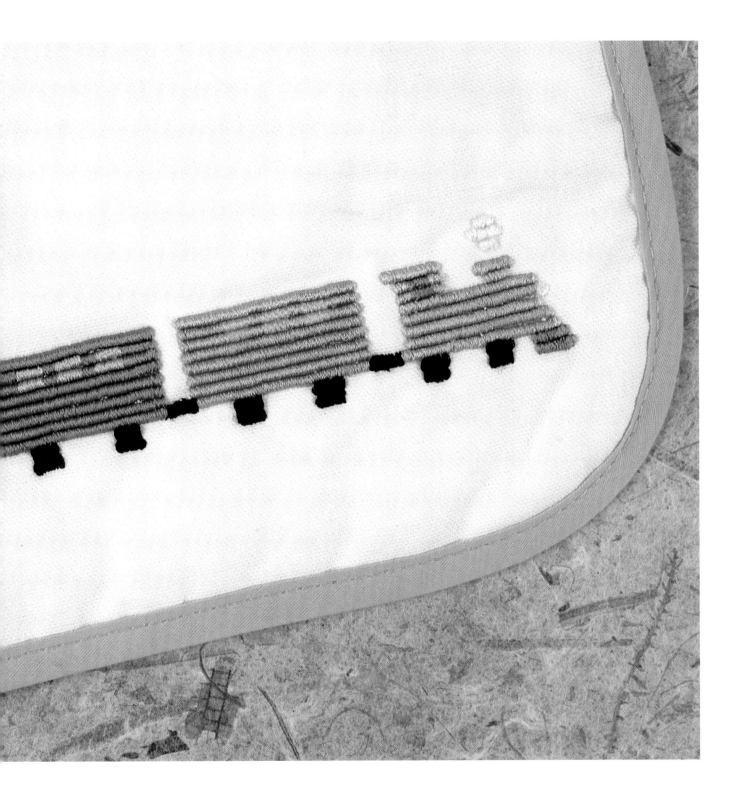

CIRCULAR EMBROIDERY

Stitching perfect rounds of colorful embroidery without the need to draw a single circle is easily achieved using a circular embroidery attachment. Although the attachment may vary in physical appearance from manufacturer to manufacturer, it operates on the same basic principle — the center of a piece of fabric is mounted on a pivot pin. This pin is adjusted a determined distance from the needle which equals the radius or half the finished circle's width. The presser foot and feed dogs move the fabric forward while pivoting on the pin in a circle. Any decorative or utility stitch can be used making the creative possibilities endless. Consider using a circular embroidery attachment for future "in-the-round" projects, such as jewelry pouches, crests and patches, curving ruffles, or folk art yo-yos!

MACHINE SET-UP

Decorative Circular Embroidery
- **Stitch:** Any straight or decorative stitch, L and W — Preset
- **Presser Foot:** Open or clear embroidery foot
- **Needles:** Match to fabric
- **Threads:** Needle — Rayon embroidery
  Bobbin — All-purpose polyester
- **Tension:** Normal to slightly tightened needle

Circular Embroidery Yo-Yos
- **Stitch:** Zig zag, L and W — 2
- **Presser Foot:** Open or clear embroidery foot
- **Needles:** Match to fabric
- **Threads:** Needle — All-purpose polyester
  Bobbin — All-purpose polyester
- **Tension:** Normal

FABRIC CHOICES:

Wovens, as desired for circular embroidery
Firmly woven fabrics are ideal for first-time yo-yo making; however, luxury fibers such as satins and taffetas may also be used

ADDITIONAL SUPPLIES:

- Cordonnet or topstitching thread, gimp or Pearl Crown Rayon
- Tear-away stabilizer
- Air- or water-soluble fabric marker
- Seam sealant
- Fine embroidery scissors

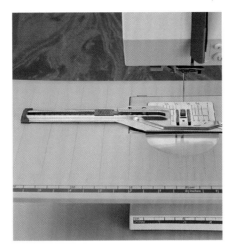

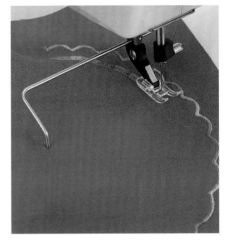

1 Cut the fabric in squares 1"–2" wider than the finished circle on all sides. Fold the squares in quarters and mark the center using a fade-away fabric marker.

2 Attach the circular embroidery attachment to your machine following the manufacturers' directions. Place the center mark of the fabric on the pivot pin.

3 For decorative circular embroidery, select any decorative stitch pattern. Sew at a slow even speed. (Note: The presser foot and feed dogs will automatically pivot the fabric around into a circular shape.)

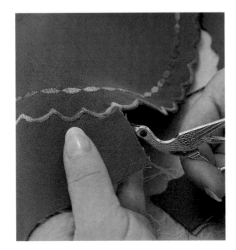

4 If your decorative stitches form an edge finish, coat the completed stitching with seam sealant to prevent fraying. Trim close to the stitches when completely dry.

continued

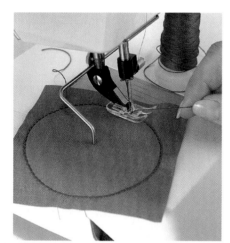

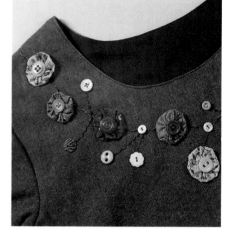

5 If creating yo-yos, place a single strand of heavy cord into the thread guide or over the front bar on your presser foot. Zig-zag over the cord, allowing the stitches to fall left and right of the cord and not catching it in the stitching. Overlap the beginning and ending points by two stitches.

6 Remove the fabric, trim the needle and bobbin threads, and then trim the excess fabric from the stitched circle, leaving a scant ¼" seam allowance. Pull the couched cord, creating a gathered circle.

7 Knot the thread tails and tuck the raw edges into the center of the yo-yo, or flip to the gathered side and cover the raw-edged center with a decorative button.

Tip As you near the starting point of your circular design, estimate how many more stitch patterns it will take to complete the circle. If necessary, fine-tune the size and number of patterns needed by either changing the stitch length or using the balance function to stretch or condense the stitch pattern.

CORDING, MONK'S CORD

Use your sewing machine to create unique, one-of-a-kind cords and bulky trims without sewing a single stitch! Following this technique, you can create custom trims to incorporate into your next garment or home decorating project.

MACHINE SET-UP

This technique makes use of the bobbin winding system on your machine.
♦ **Threads:** Thick or thin cords, threads, yarns, mini-braids, or other miscellaneous thread-y fibers

ADDITIONAL SUPPLIES:

♦ Empty bobbin
♦ Optional: Dental floss threader

1 Measure three times the desired finished length of cord. Select at least 3–4 cords for interest and to create a bulky braid. (Note: As a rule, you can't cut the cords any longer than what you can tautly hold an arm's length from the bobbin spool pin on the sewing machine. You will also need to be able to reach the presser foot of your machine in order to twist the cords.)

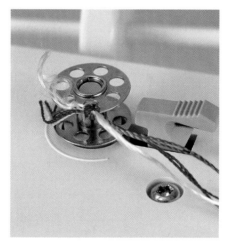

2 Draw all the cords through a hole on the bobbin. Bring the cords from the inside, near the center post, up through to the top of the bobbin. Knot your cords at least twice, with the knot resting on the top of the bobbin.

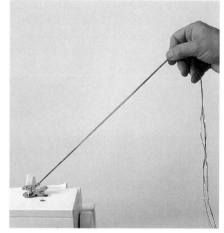

3 Place the bobbin on the bobbin winder pin. Hold all the cords tautly in one hand at a slight 45-degree angle.

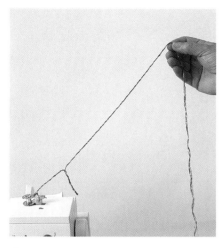 

4 Engage the bobbin winder and press down on the foot pedal. The cords held in your hand will begin to twist. Stop winding when you feel a slight tension and the cords begin to pull in.

5 Using your free hand, pinch the twisted cords in the center. Bring the loose cord tail ends that are held in your other hand down to meet and touch the knot on the bobbin. Hold the cord tails and those knotted to the bobbin in one hand. Release the center point held in your other hand. The twisted and doubled cord will wrap around itself, creating a unique and beautiful corded trim. Run the cord between your thumb and index finger to smooth out. Clip the cord tails from the bobbin and knot securely.

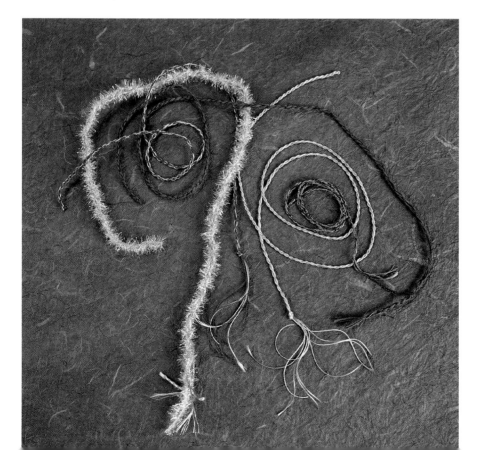

CORDING, ON SCALLOPED EDGES

Frequently sewers are disappointed with the finished look of a machine-sewn scalloped edge. Usually the satin-stitched finish looks perfect before trimming but seems irregular and unprofessional afterwards. The reason for this irregular edge is in the trimming away of excess fabric. Cut too close and you risk snipping into the satin stitching; cut too far away and your scallops now have that "loving hands at home" look. Remedy this dilemma by couching a cord onto the trimmed fabric edge along the outside of the scallop. Not only does this give an elegant, clean finished look to the scallop, but allows the sewer a bit more breathing room while trimming.

MACHINE SET-UP

- ♦ **Stitch:** Zig zag, L and W — approximately 1½
- ♦ **Presser Foot:** Foot with guide for couching cord
- ♦ **Needles:** Universal needle, size #70 or #80
- ♦ **Threads:** Needle and bobbin — Rayon or cotton embroidery, color matched to satin stitching
- ♦ **Tension:** Normal

FABRIC CHOICES:

Woven fabrics, all weights

ADDITIONAL SUPPLIES:

- ♦ Seam sealant
- ♦ Fine embroidery scissors
- ♦ Couching cord for the edge, such as Perle Cotton, Pearl Crown Rayon, embroidery floss or topstitching thread

1 This technique begins after the scalloped edge has been sewn. Apply seam sealant to the scallop embroidered edge. Trim the sewn edge close to the scallop, leaving a scant ⅛" fabric edge. This narrow edge will easily be covered by the couched cord and produce a fine edge finish.

2 Place the couching cord into the guide on the presser foot and position the loaded foot onto the first trimmed scallop edge. Begin to sew a zig zag over the trimmed edge. The left swing of the zig zag should fall into the satin-stitched edge of the scallop; the right swing of the zig zag should fall completely off the edge.

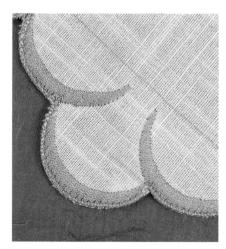

3 The filler cord will be caught in the zig zag stitches, filling in and covering the cut edges.

COUCHING, BEADS AND SEQUINS

Adding sparkle to any sewing project is easily achieved with a simple zig zag stitch, the proper presser foot, and beautiful strands of beads or sequins. Adding elegant, glittering accents to bridal gowns and evening wear, as well as, holiday projects, is easy with a few simple guidelines. The strands of beads or sequins are stitched over to secure them to the fabric. A clear nylon thread is usually used hiding inconspicuously between the beads or sequins. Straight lines or gentle curves work best with this technique.

MACHINE SET-UP

- **Stitch:** Zig zag, L and W — adjusted to the size of the beads or sequins being used
- **Presser Foot:** For Beads — Piping or bulky overlock foot with a deep groove for feeding strung beads and pearls
  For Sequins — Embroidery or appliqué, sequin, or slotted foot with an indented sole and opening wide enough to allow sequins to pass smoothly underneath
- **Needles:** Match to fabric
- **Threads:** Needle — Monofilament
  Bobbin — All-purpose polyester, color matched to base fabric
- **Tension:** Normal
- **Optional:** Engage needle down function

FABRIC CHOICES:

As desired

ADDITIONAL SUPPLIES:

- Air- or water-soluble fabric marker
- Fusible interfacing
- Lightweight, tear-away stabilizer
- Seam sealant
- Optional: Fabric glue

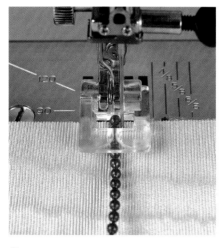

1 Follow Steps 1 and 2 in "Couching, Cords, Braids, and Bulky Fibers" to prepare the fabric. Mark the design lines to follow using a fabric marker. Select the appropriate-size foot for the beads or sequins size chosen.

2 Place the beads under the foot leaving a 4" tail in the back. Place a layer of tear-away stabilizer underneath the area to be couched. Adjust the stitch width to just pass over the beads.

3 Continue stitching until all lines of the design are beaded. Clip the strand between the beads at the end of the stitching. If the design is in the middle of the fabric, clip the strand and place a dot of fabric glue under the last bead to secure it.

continued

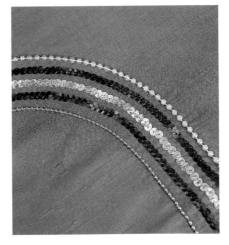

4 For sequins, select a foot that will allow the sequins to slide smoothly under the foot with the "nap" facing forward. If the sequins are placed in the opposite direction, you risk the sequins catching on the foot and breaking. (Note: Sequins are made of plastic. Should you accidentally pierce a sequin while sewing, your needle will dull but not break. Replace the needle when you are finished couching the strand.)

5 When the couching is complete, remove the tear-away stabilizer. Remove a few sequins from the end and dot the thread tails with seam sealant. Draw the tails to the wrong side when dry.

Tip It is usually best to start and stop the couching within the seam allowances so the beginning and ending points don't show.

For smooth curves, stop and pivot frequently, lifting the foot slightly to release the fabric and re-position the beads or sequins.

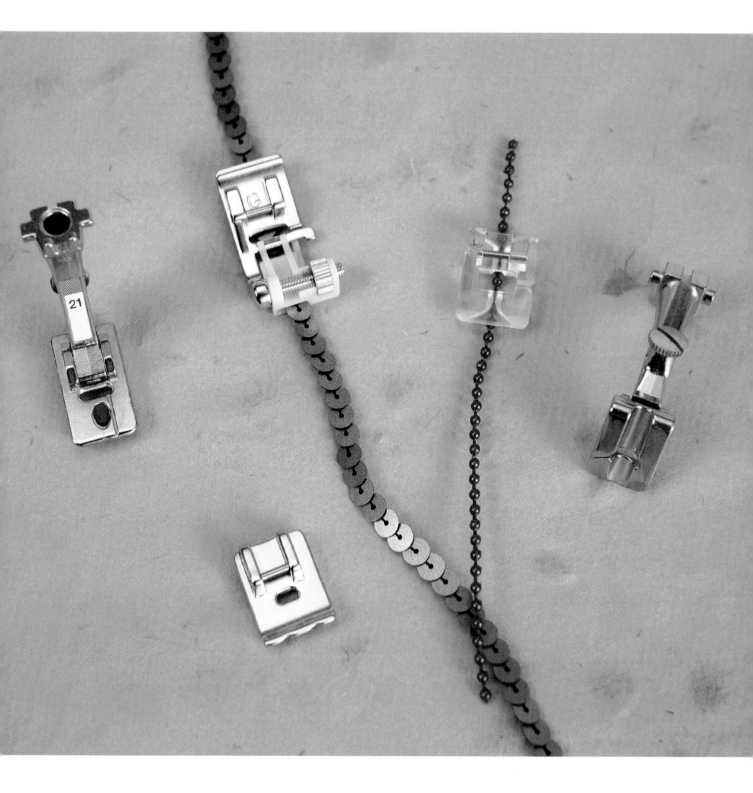

COUCHING, CORDS, BRAIDS, AND BULKY FIBERS

A hand-embroidery term that means stitching over cord, couching is easily adapted to the sewing machine as an embellishment technique. Any stitch that has a side-to-side motion, such as a zig zag or feather stitch, can be used to attach cord, yarn, or decorative threads to the surface of the fabric. Select a presser foot designed to allow the cords to move freely with either a hole in the front or a tunnel on the underside holding it in place while being stitched.

Change the look of your finished embellishment by selecting different needle threads and decorative stitches. Match the color of the needle thread to the base fabric to make the cord appear woven into it. Use a contrasting color or monofilament to make the cord appear to float on the fabric surface. Experiment to find the right look.

MACHINE SET-UP

♦ **Stitch:** Zig zag or decorative stitch, L and W — adjusted to the specific fibers chosen for couching
♦ **Presser Foot:** Piping foot or cording feet
♦ **Needles:** Match to fabric. Metafil needles for all metallic threads
♦ **Threads:** Needle — Monofilament for invisible couching, metallics or rayons for color interest. Bobbin — All-purpose polyester, color matched to base fabric
♦ **Tension:** Normal
♦ **Optional:** Engage needle down function

FABRIC CHOICES:

Any woven fabric or stable knits

ADDITIONAL SUPPLIES:

♦ Cotton, rayon or metallic, thick or thin cords, yarns or braids, rat tail cording, multiple strands of sewing thread
♦ Air- or water-soluble fabric marker
♦ Optional: Tear-away stabilizer or fusible interfacing

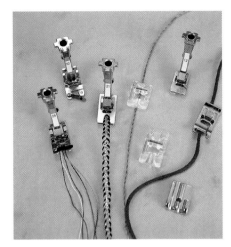

1 Fuse a piece of interfacing to the wrong side of the area to be embellished. Using a fabric marker, draw the design guidelines to follow when sewing.

2 Select the appropriate presser foot to match the materials being couched.

3 Attach the loaded presser foot to the machine, leaving a 3"–4" tail of excess cord behind the foot to help the feeding at the start of sewing. Place the fabric under the foot centering it on the drawn line. Select the desired stitch, making sure the stitch width will cover slightly or just pierce the cords. Begin to sew at a slow, even speed for the best results.

Tip It is best to start and stop in a seam allowance whenever possible. If this is not available, leave a 4–6" tail of cord at the beginning and end of the couching. This tail can be pulled to the wrong side using a large-eye needle and secured. Dot all fiber ends with seam sealant and clip when dry.

CRISSCROSS CHAIN STITCHING

Duplicate the look of a hand-embroidered chain stitch effortlessly with your sewing machine. Use these delicate crossed and stitched loops of thread, ribbon, or cording, as vine greenery, background filler, or meandering traces of color added for surface interest. Any thread, heavy cord, or ribbon that won't pass through the eye of a needle is suitable for this technique.

MACHINE SET-UP

- **Stitch:** Straight, L — 2–5 depending on the size of chain desired
- **Presser Foot:** Open embroidery foot
- **Needles:** Appropriate to fabric chosen
- **Threads:** Needle — Monofilament
  Bobbin — All-purpose polyester, color matched to base fabric
- **Tension:** Normal
- **Optional:** Engage needle down function

FABRIC CHOICES:

Medium- to heavy-weight wovens best; however, firm knits can also be used if interfaced well

ADDITIONAL SUPPLIES:

- Air-soluble or fabric chalk marker
- Heavy decorative threads such as perle cotton, Glamour™, Decor™, Ribbon Floss™, or silk ribbons
- Lightweight, woven interfacing

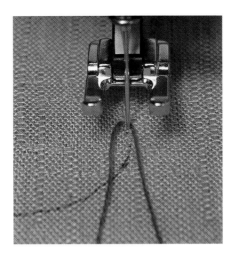

1 Fuse the interfacing to the wrong side of the area to be stitched. Using a fabric marking tool, trace your desired design for the chain stitching. Cut the decorative thread or cord to be used approximately 2½ times the length of the drawn design.

2 At the beginning of the design, sew a few stitches back and forth into the fabric to secure the slippery monofilament thread. With the needle down in the fabric, raise the presser foot and wrap the decorative cord around the needle bringing the tails to the front making sure both sides are equal in length.

3 Lower the presser foot and sew back and forth over the center point of the cord to secure it to the fabric. Keep the cord tails away from the needle.

4 Sew forward two stitches. Cross the left and right cords across the front of the needle forming a loop. With the cords crossed, sew over the intersection, forming one chain link.

continued

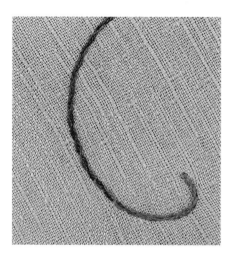

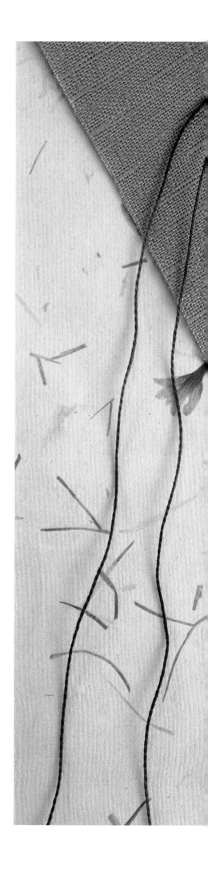

5 Repeat sewing and crossing, remembering to keep the cord tails away from the needle until the crisscrossing. This process will create a hand-look chain stitch. Leave a 6" tail of extra cord at the end of the design line. Draw these cords to the wrong side using a hand tapestry needle. Knot the tails and clip.

Tip Experiment with different stitch lengths and the number of stitches sewn before crossing the cords. Try coordinating or contrasting different colored cords to add subtle or striking accents.

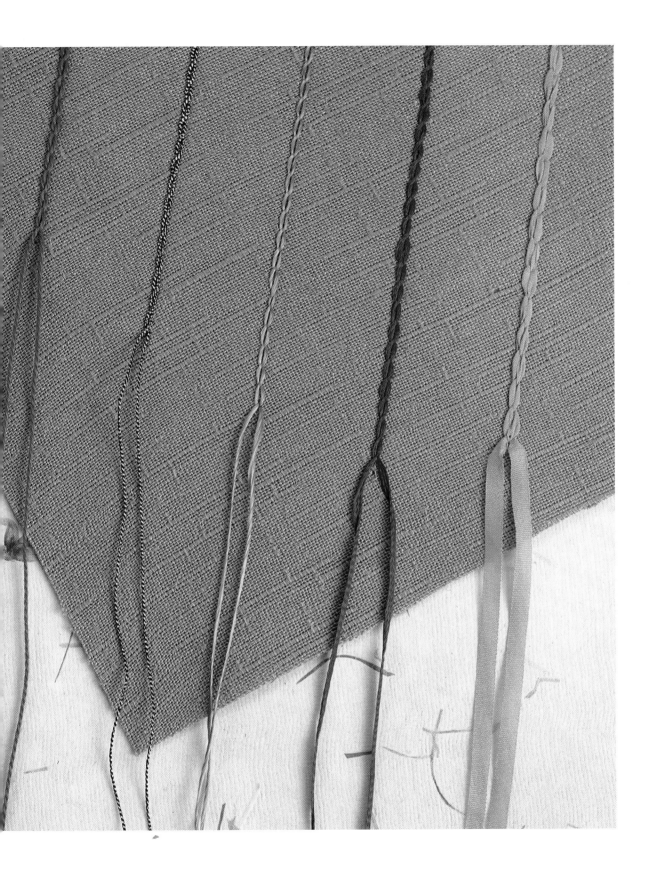

CUTWORK

Cutwork is often defined as an embroidery technique with areas of fabric cut away and the raw edges over-sewn with embroidery thread. This hand technique has become a very popular sewing machine technique with elegant cutwork designs being created in fine fabrics. Embroidered bars, such as those used for Batternburg lace, are added to connect larger open areas. Add cutwork to jackets, vests, and blouses, as well as, beautiful table linens.

MACHINE SET-UP

- ♦ **Stitch:** Step One: Straight
  Step Two: Zig zag, W — 1
  Step Three: Zig zag, W — 2
  Step Four: Zig zag, W — 2–4 based on the size of the design
- ♦ **Presser Foot:** Darning or free-motion foot
- ♦ **Needles:** Universal needle, size #70 or #80
- ♦ **Threads:** Needle and bobbin — 40 wt. or 60 wt. cotton embroidery
- ♦ **Tension:** Adjust needle as necessary
- ♦ **Feed Dogs:** Lowered
- ♦ **Optional:** Adjust presser foot pressure for free-motion work

FABRIC CHOICES:

Firm fabrics such as linen, silk, heavier cottons

ADDITIONAL SUPPLIES:

- ♦ Water-soluble stabilizer
- ♦ Spring-loaded or cotton embroidery hoop
- ♦ Air- or water-soluble fabric marker
- ♦ Embroidery or appliqué scissors
- ♦ Optional: Temporary spray adhesive

1 Trace your design with the marking pen directly onto the fabric. Mark the areas to be cut away with an "X". Layer the fabric over the water-soluble stabilizer and insert into the hoop. Make sure the fabric and stabilizer are taut.

2 Outline your design using the settings for Step One. Outline the design a second time using the settings for Step Two.

3 Carefully cut away the layer of fabric in the marked areas without removing the water-soluble stabilizer. (Note: It is often best to complete the design in sections, cutting away small areas one at a time.)

4 To create the filler bars, set your machine to a straight stitch. Secure the needle and bobbin threads at one edge of the cut area. Slightly raise the presser foot and move across the open area with your needle. Secure the threads on the opposite side. Go back and forth in the same place two or three times.

5 Oversew these "floating" threads using the settings in Step Three to create a solid bar. Move the hoop at a constant speed to produce an even satin stitch.

continued

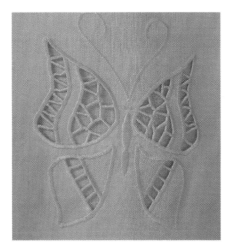

6 Satin-stitch around all the raw edges adjusting the width of the zig zag according to the size of the design.

7 The filler bars can also be designed in a spider web-like effect for a different appearance. Carefully remove the water-soluble stabilizer from the finished cutwork design.

Tip Using a temporary spray adhesive, adhere two layers of water-soluble stabilizer together producing a heavier stabilizer. You can also adhere the water-soluble stabilizer directly to your fabric to avoid any slipping or sliding.

DRAWN THREADWORK

Drawn threadwork is an interesting technique utilizing the weave of the fabric as well as decorative stitching. Crosswise threads are pulled and then oversewn to create this interesting detail. You will often find drawn work on elegant table linens and napkins.

MACHINE SET-UP

- **Stitch:** Step One: Zig zag, L — 1½, W — 1½
  Step Two: Zig zag, L — N/A, W — 1½–2
  Step Three: Zig zag, L — ½, W — 2–2½
- **Presser Foot:** All-purpose foot and darning or free-motion foot
- **Needles:** Match to fabric
- **Threads:** Needle and bobbin — Cotton or rayon embroidery
- **Tension:** Normal
- **Feed Dogs:** Lowered for Step 3
- **Optional:** Engage needle down function

FABRIC CHOICES:

Nubby fabrics with heavier crosswise threads, such as linen or silk

ADDITIONAL SUPPLIES:

- Spring-loaded or wooden embroidery hoop

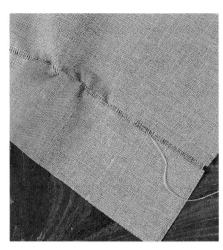  

1 Determine where the design will be placed. Find the straight of grain and begin pulling crosswise threads from the fabric. Pull threads to the width desired. Center the drawn area in your embroidery hoop.

2 Using a narrow zig zag, stitch along each edge of the drawn area. Knot the threads tails at each end.

3 Lower the feed dogs, attach the darning foot, and adjust the machine settings for Step Two. Beginning on the edge of the drawn area, start zig zagging over the remaining lengthwise threads. (Note: These loose threads will draw in together with the wider zig zag.)

4 Once the lengthwise threads are oversewn, finish the outer edges using Step Three settings.

continued

Tip When oversewing the lengthwise threads, keep the hoop moving at a steady pace so the satin stitching is even.

For best results, work in small sections at a time.

EMBROIDERY, FREE-MOTION

Free-motion embroidery is literally like drawing with your sewing machine. Only a straight or zig zag stitch is necessary to fill in your designs. Expand your embroidery repertoire beyond the built-in stitches or computerized designs already on your machine. Experiment with different threads and stitching techniques to vary the look of the finished design.

MACHINE SET-UP

- **Stitch:** Straight
- **Presser Foot:** Darning or free-motion foot, or no foot
- **Needles:** Embroidery needle, size matched to thread
- **Threads:** Needle — cotton or rayon embroidery, metallic, silk
  Bobbin — 60 wt. cotton embroidery
- **Tension:** Loosen needle
- **Feed Dogs:** Lowered
- **Optional:** Engage needle down function or adjust presser foot pressure for free-motion work

FABRIC CHOICES:

Firmly woven fabrics of all weights work best
Knits and loosely woven fabrics need to be stabilized

ADDITIONAL SUPPLIES:

- Tear-away stabilizer
- Air- or water-soluble fabric marker
- Spring-loaded or wooden embroidery hoop

1 Using your marking pen, draw the design on the fabric. Place the fabric in the embroidery hoop making sure it is taut. Place a layer of tear-away stabilizer under the hoop. Lower the feed dogs and thread the machine with your thread of choice.

2 Holding the hoop firmly on each side with your fingers, begin stitching the vine moving back and forth along the marked line giving the stems some dimension.

3 Outline the leaves and then fill in the center in the same manner. Only moving the hoop back and forth or right and left will keep the direction of your stitches all going in the same way.

4 For added texture, move the hoop in a circular, swirling motion to fill in the petals of the flowers. This technique creates a light, airy effect on your design.

5 Fill in the centers of any flowers as the last step. Tie off all threads on the back.

Tip Stitch at a constant medium speed — not too fast and not too slow. Practice on a sample first to get into the "rhythm".

ENTREDEUX, BASIC

Entredeux is a French term that literally translates to mean "between two". The entredeux used extensively in heirloom sewing is a narrow band of commercially embroidered trim. It resembles a tiny ladder sewn on very crisp batiste. It is often used as a bridging trim, therefore the reference to "between two", to strengthen multiple rows of delicate laces. Because of its dominating presence in heirloom projects, using purchased entredeux can greatly add to the overall cost of your project. Consider making your own entredeux trim by using a wing needle and batiste fabric.

The side extensions found on the wing needle make an extra large hole in the fabric, which is kept open by the tension on the needle and bobbin threads of the chosen decorative stitch. Select a stitch pattern that sews multiple times in the same place. Some sewing machine models have a pre-programmed stitch designed especially for creating entredeux embroidery. Besides the cost benefit by making your own entredeux, home sewers are no longer limited to the basic white or ecru colors of factory-produced entredeux. All the colors in the rainbow for both threads and fabrics are yours for the choosing!

MACHINE SET-UP

- **Stitch:** Daisy/star stitch or pre-programmed entredeux; L and W — approximately 2
- **Presser Foot:** All-purpose or open embroidery foot
- **Needles:** Single wing needle, size #100–110
- **Threads:** Needle — 30 or 40 wt. rayon or 60 wt. cotton embroidery
  Bobbin — 60 wt. cotton embroidery
- **Tension:** Normal
- **Optional:** Engage wing needle limitation, if available

FABRIC CHOICES:

Natural fiber fabrics preferred, all-cotton batiste, organdy or linens

ADDITIONAL SUPPLIES:

- Fabric spray starch
- Optional: Crisp tear-away stabilizer

1 Mist the single layer of fabric to be sewn with starch; iron dry. Repeat several times until the base fabric is quite crisp. Draw a guideline through the center of the fabric.

2 Center the presser foot over the drawn line. Begin to stitch slowly, noting that the holes from the needle are being kept open by both the needle and bobbin threads. Continue to stitch down the length of the fabric.

3 Trim and press when complete.

ENTREDEUX, CORDED

Sew a more defined edge on your embroidered entredeux trim by including fine cords on the left and right sides of the stitching. Choose special presser feet to guide the cords while stitching, adding a raised edge to your band of elegant entredeux.

MACHINE SET-UP

- ♦ **Stitch:** Daisy/star stitch, pre-programmed entredeux
- ♦ **Presser Foot:** Multi-grooved cording foot
- ♦ **Needles:** Single wing needle, size #100–110
- ♦ **Threads:** Refer to "Entredeux, Basic"
- ♦ **Tension:** Normal
- ♦ **Optional:** Engage wing needle limitation, if available

FABRIC CHOICES:

Same as in "Entredeux, Basic"

ADDITIONAL SUPPLIES:

- ♦ Spray starch
- ♦ Gimp or topstitching thread
- ♦ Optional: Crisp, tear-away stabilizer

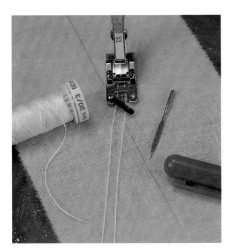

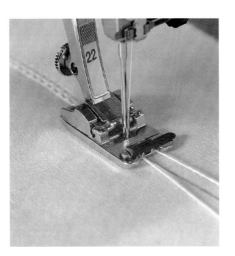

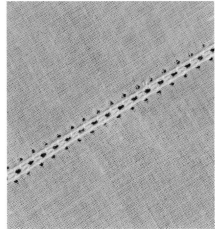

1 Pretreat the fabric as in "Entredeux, Basic". Cut two pieces of filler cord slightly longer than the band of entredeux trim to be sewn. Load the filler cord into the presser foot. The grooves chosen should correspond to the left and right hand swing of the stitch.

2 Center the presser foot on the drawn line on the fabric to be stitched. Adjust the cords to flow smoothly in front of the foot. Slowly begin to sew the corded entredeux, making sure that the left- and right-hand stitches catch the filler cord.

3 Continue to sew down the length of the fabric.

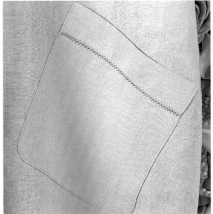

4 Trim and press when complete.

EYELET EMBROIDERY

A unique embellishment, eyelets are actually holes embroidered into the fabric. Machine-sewn eyelets can be quite versatile. They can be utilitarian, replacing buttonholes for closing garments or as a decorative embellishment with additional stitches turning the holes into fantasy flowers or fringed eyes on animal projects. Ethnic embroideries with shisha mirror inserts can even be duplicated with this eyelet technique.

MACHINE SET-UP

- **Stitch:** Step One: Zig zag, W — 1½–2; Step Two: Zig zag, W — 4–5
- **Presser Foot:** Eyelet attachment and recommended foot
- **Needles:** Match to fabric
- **Threads:** Needle and bobbin — Cotton or rayon embroidery
- **Tension:** Step One: Normal Step Two: Slightly lowered needle
- **Feed Dogs:** Lowered

FABRIC CHOICES:

Tightly woven medium-weight wovens

ADDITIONAL SUPPLIES:

- Spring-loaded or wooden embroidery hoop
- Weft insertion interfacing

1 Fuse the interfacing to the wrong side of the area designated for eyelets. Place the fabric in the embroidery hoop keeping the fabric taut. Using a block and cutter or awl, create a small hole in the fabric for the first eyelet. (Note: Due to the sideways motion of the zig zag stitch encircling the hole, the opening will always finish larger than cut. Keep this in mind before cutting open the hole.)

2 Position the cut hole on the post of the eyelet maker attached to the sewing machine.

3 Set the machine according to the settings in Machine Set-Up. Sew the first row of securing zig zag stitches, pivoting the hoop around the center post to satin-stitch a circle.

4 Reset the sewing machine for a wider zig zag. Oversew the first ring of zig zag stitches. At the end of the second stitching, reduce the stitch width to 0. Sew 3–4 stitches in place creating a securing knot.

continued

5 Enhance plain eyelets by replacing the wide zig zag stitches with decorative stitches. Turn basic eyelets into delightful flowers or doll face eyes and noses. Replace the second row of zig zag stitches with a half scallop, half triangle or any other decorative stitch. Move the hoop slowly, pivoting carefully to retain the shape of the decorative stitch.

6 To sew fringed eyelets, follow the directions for Machine Set-Up for the first and second rows of zig zag stitches. Zig-zag a third time, using a width of 2. Using a small pair of sharp-tipped embroidery scissors, clip the outer edge of the stitches, creating a fluffy fringe around the securing satin stitching.

Tip Create eyelets with a special attachment or tool recommended by your specific machine manufacturer. Most attachments have the capability of making multi-sized eyelets.

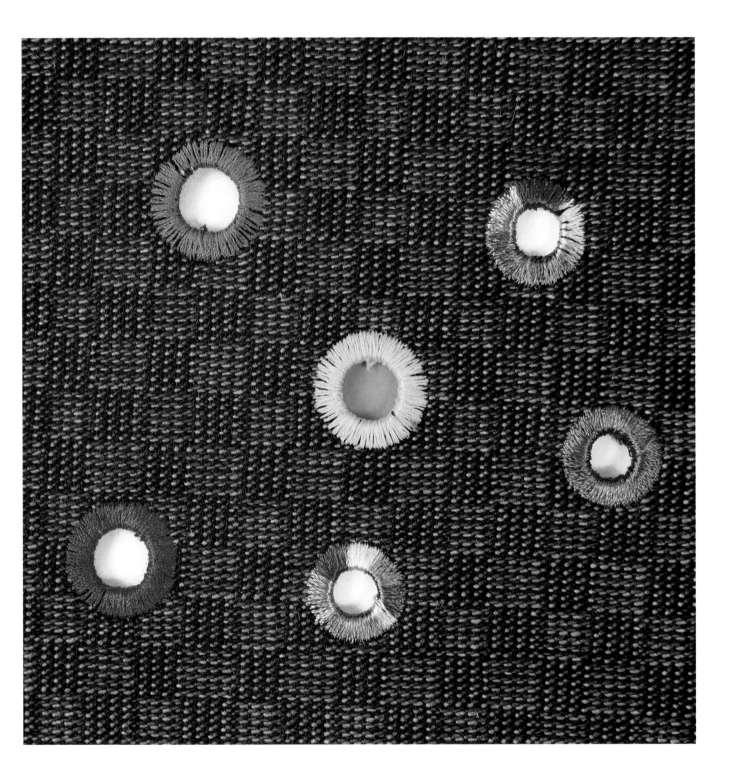

FAGOTING, BOBBINWORK

Traditional fagoting can have a dramatic change in appearance when the normal bobbin thread is replaced with a heavier cord. Switch to a secondary bobbin case, fill your bobbin with Pearl Crown Rayon, and try this handwork look-alike on your machine.

MACHINE SET-UP

♦ **Stitch:** Feather or briar stitch or other bridging stitch of choice, L — 2–3, W — 4 or wider
♦ **Presser Foot:** Open or clear embroidery foot
♦ **Needles:** Match to fabric
♦ **Threads:** Needle — All-purpose polyester, color-matched to the bobbin thread
   Bobbin — Heavier cord, such as Pearl Crown Rayon or buttonhole twist
♦ **Tension:** Needle — Normal to moderately tightened
   Bobbin — Loosened to feed freely

FABRIC CHOICES:

Light- to medium weight woven fabrics

ADDITIONAL SUPPLIES:

♦ Fagoting needle plate or plastic coffee stirrer
♦ Spray starch

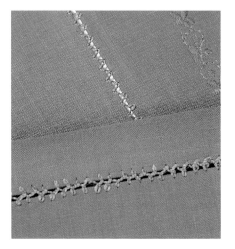

1 Prepare fabrics as for "Fagoting, Traditional". Wind the bobbin with heavier cord. Adjust or bypass the bobbin tension according to your machine manual. Place the fabrics, wrong side up, on the sewing machine. The decorative stitches will be formed from the wrong side.

2 With the fabrics placed on either side of the fagoting plate or coffee stirrer, begin to sew at a slow, even pace. The left- and right-hand swing of the stitch pattern will sew into the folded fabric edges.

FAGOTING, BUNDLED

An entirely different decorative look, also called fagoting, can be achieved with an easy three-step process. Stitches are sewn, bundled down the center, and then decoratively edged. Highly decorative, and far easier than it appears, it's a definite "must have" among your list of sewing techniques.

MACHINE SET-UP

- **Stitch:** Step One: Zig zag , L — $\frac{1}{2}$, W — 4–5
  Step Two: Triple straight stitch, L — 3–4
  Step Three: Any decorative stitch, preset
- **Presser Foot:** Step One: Tailor tack or fringing foot
  Step Two: Open or clear embroidery foot
  Step Three: Open or clear embroidery foot
- **Needles:** Match to fabric
- **Threads:** Needle and bobbin — Cotton or rayon embroidery thread
- **Tension:** Step One: 1–1$\frac{1}{2}$
  Step Two: Normal
  Step Three: Normal

FABRIC CHOICES:

Light- to medium weight woven fabrics

ADDITIONAL SUPPLIES:

- Spray starch

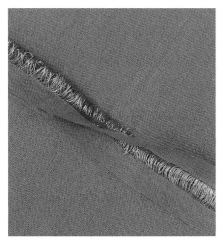

1 Lightly spray-starch the fabrics. Draw a stitching line at least ⅝" away from the cut fabric edge.

2 With right sides together, sew two layers of fabric together along the drawn line.

3 Carefully pull the seam apart, revealing a vertical band of horizontal stitches. Press the seam allowances away from the stitches.

4 Reset the sewing machine for Step Two. (Note: It is critical to remember to return the needle tension to a normal setting.) While holding the pressed edges as far apart as possible, begin to sew down the center of the thread fagoting. The forward and backward motion of the triple straight stitch will form tiny bow-like bundles of stitches.

5 Adjust the machine for Step Three and select any decorative stitch. Sew along the left and right edges of the fagoting, securing the row of fagoting stitches.

FAGOTING, TRADITIONAL

Fagoting is a beautiful option for joining two pieces of fabric. This fabric-bridging technique features stitches sewn partially on and off clean-finished fabric edges. It can be used for practical purposes, such as adding length to a child's dress, or decoratively accenting a blouse collar, cuffs or front placket. Duplicating a hand technique, fagoting can have many different looks depending upon the types of threads chosen for your stitching.

MACHINE SET-UP

♦ **Stitch:** Feather stitch, L — 1½–2½, W — 4 or wider
♦ **Presser Foot:** Open or clear embroidery foot
♦ **Needles:** Match to fabric
♦ **Threads:** Needle and bobbin — Cotton or rayon embroidery
♦ **Tension:** Loosen needle

FABRIC CHOICES:

Light- to medium weight woven fabrics

ADDITIONAL SUPPLIES:

♦ Fagoting needle plate or plastic coffee stirrer
♦ Spray starch

 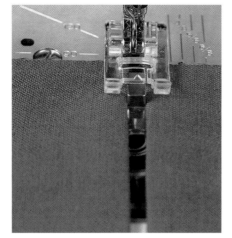 

1 Clean-finish both the edges that are to be joined with the bridging stitch. Mist and iron-dry the fabric edges if the fabric is extremely soft. Tape a coffee stirrer to the bed of the sewing machine, centered in front of the needle plate, or use the fagoting needle plate appropriate to your machine. This will help guide the fabric edges.

2 Position each layer of fabric to the left and right of the pins on the needle plate or the coffee stirrer guide. Select the feather stitch.

3 Begin to sew the feather stitching, catching the left- and right-hand folded edges. The center of the stitch will sew on the open area created by the guide. Complete stitching along the entire length of the fabric.

FOLDED FLOURISHES, PRAIRIE POINTS

Prairie points are quick and easy to make and provide endless design variations in how they are folded and pieced into a project. Most often seen as an edge-finishing detail on quilts and wall hangings, prairie points can also be found tucked into garment seams or on the edges of home decorating projects, such as pillows and country-style window treatments.

MACHINE SET-UP

♦ **Stitch:** Straight, L — 2½
♦ **Presser Foot:** All-purpose foot
♦ **Needles:** Universal needle, size #80
♦ **Threads:** Needle and bobbin — All-purpose polyester
♦ **Tension:** Normal

FABRIC CHOICES:

Light- to medium weight woven fabrics, cottons, linens, satins, and silks, or metallic, such as lamé

ADDITIONAL SUPPLIES:

♦ Rotary cutter and mat

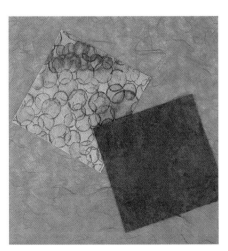  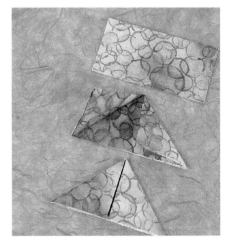

1 Cut the squares of fabric in the size desired for the finished points. Press flat to assure the most accurate folding.

2 For an open-sided prairie point, fold the square in half diagonally. Fold the triangle in half diagonally again.

3 For an inside-fold prairie point, fold the square in half. From a center point along the folded edge, fold the corners diagonally down to the center.

continued

4 To sew multiple open-sided prairie points into a seam, slip one point partially inside the open end of an adjacent point as far as desired. Pin and continue to create a strip of points.

5 For inside-fold points, place each point side by side with the narrow ends overlapping edges as far as desired. Pin and continue to create the band. Baste the pieces together if desired.

6 Place the pinned band, right sides down, along the raw edge of the seam to be embellished. Place the appropriate layer of fabric on top of the band and sew the seam, encasing the prairie point accent trim between the fabric layers.

Tip Prairie points are always created from squares of fabric; the size used is up to you. Any size square will work for the two basic techniques discussed here.

FOLDED FLOURISHES, SHARK'S TEETH

Add an understated geometric touch to your next sewing project by sewing in rows of folded and stitched points called shark's teeth. Borrowed from the world of heirloom sewing, these delicate, folded points appear much harder to sew than they actually are. The key to perfect shark's teeth is heavily starched or crisp fabric making the sewing and snipping as easy as possible. Creating these embellishments is a simple process of sewing the tuck, marking and clipping the fold, pressing and stitching again. A steady hand and sharp-tipped embroidery scissors, plus a special tuck guide ruler, are all you need to be able to add this delightful accent to your next garment hem, cuffs, or bodice front.

MACHINE SET-UP

- ♦ **Stitch:** Straight, L — 2; Zig zag, L and W — approximately 1½–2
- ♦ **Presser Foot:** All-purpose foot with quilting guide
- ♦ **Needles:** Universal needle, size #60 or #70
- ♦ **Threads:** Needle and bobbin — 60 wt. cotton embroidery
- ♦ **Tension:** Normal
- ♦ **Optional:** Engage needle down function

FABRIC CHOICES:

Lightweight, all-natural fibers preferred, such as cotton batiste, linen, and cotton organdy

ADDITIONAL SUPPLIES:

- ♦ Tuck and point ruler or clear plastic ruler for tuck and clip marking
- ♦ Fine-tipped embroidery scissors
- ♦ Air- or water-soluble fabric marker
- ♦ Spray starch

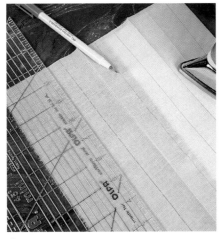

1 To assure that your fabric is on grain and to prevent distorting, pull a few fiber threads and cut the fabric to be tucked along this thread channel. This will assure that your fabric is on grain and prevent distorting. Heavily spray starch and iron the fabric dry many times.

2 Lightly mark straight and parallel rows for tucks across the fabric. Crease mark the tucks to be sewn, using an iron.

3 To assure straight and even sewing, attach an adjustable seam guide to the sewing machine or presser foot to help gauge your tuck depth. Using a short, straight stitch, sew in each tuck, then press the tucks in one direction. Press again in the opposite direction to assure a crisp, non-folded line.

4 Using a clear plastic or dedicated tuck and point ruler, made especially for this technique, mark in the lines for snipping. Each row should have clip marks about halfway in between the previous row's marks.

continued

119

5 Using sharp embroidery scissors, clip on the marked lines through the tuck to within one thread of the sewn line.

6 Fold back and press the clipped edges, placing the cut edge even with the sewn tuck line. This will create a diagonal fold on each side of the clip mark and create the shark's teeth effect.

7 Reset the sewing machine for a zig zag stitch. Remove the seam guide from the presser foot and carefully zig-zag close to the straight stitching, catching the raw edges of the folded sections.

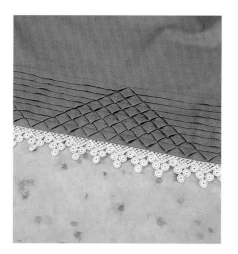

Tip To keep the grainline straight and avoid fabric distortion, alternate sewing each row of tucks from opposite ends.

FRINGE, LONG

Sewing extra long fringe is just as easy as creating its shorter form. A different sequence of steps using the same presser feet will create entirely different results.

MACHINE SET-UP

- **Stitch:** Step One: Zig zag, L — ½, W — 4
  Step Two: Any straight-sided decorative stitch, L and W — Preset
- **Presser Foot:** Step One: Tailor tack or fringing foot
  Step Two: Open or clear embroidery foot
- **Needles:** Match to fabric
- **Threads:** Needle and bobbin — Cotton or rayon embroidery
- **Tension:** Step One: Needle — 1
  Step Two: Normal

FABRIC CHOICES:

Light- to medium weight woven fabrics

ADDITIONAL SUPPLIES:

- Spray starch
- Fine embroidery scissors
- Tear-away stabilizer

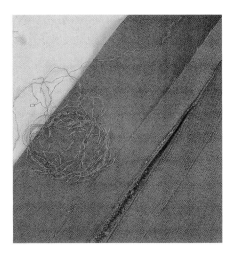

1 Press under a hem edge on both the project fabric and the anchor fabric. Position the folded fabric edges to the left and right of the center blade of the tailor tack or fringing foot. Zig-zag onto each folded edge.

2 Carefully remove the bobbin thread from the stitching. Do not pull the fabrics completely apart but flatten gently.

3 Reset the sewing machine and attach the foot for Step Two. Sew a straight-edged decorative stitch close to the fringed edge of the project fabric. This line of sewing will anchor the stitches. Remember to place a layer of tear-away stabilizer underneath the project fabric if necessary.

4 Carefully pull away the anchor fabric. Clip the loops of the fringe if desired. Remove the tear-away stabilizer and trim the hem allowance from the wrong side.

Tips You will be working with two pieces of fabric when sewing the long fringe — the project fabric and an anchor piece to be discarded.

FRINGE, SHORT

Stitching custom-colored, looped fringe on any project is as easy as sewing a zig zag stitch. Use the raised blade of the tailor tack or fringing foot to do all the work for you. Two different methods are described here to give both short and long fringed effects.

MACHINE SET-UP

- ♦ **Stitch:** Step One: Zig zag, W — 2–4, L — ½
   Step Two: Decorative satin stitch, L and W — Preset
- ♦ **Presser Foot:** Step One: Tailor tack or fringing foot
   Step Two: Open or clear embroidery foot
- ♦ **Needles:** Match to fabric
- ♦ **Threads:** Needle and bobbin — Cotton or rayon embroidery
- ♦ **Tension:** Step One: Very loose needle — 1 or 2
   Step Two: Normal

FABRIC CHOICES:

Light- to medium weight woven fabrics

ADDITIONAL SUPPLIES:

- ♦ Spray starch
- ♦ Fine embroidery scissors
- ♦ Tear-away stabilizer

1 Iron a crease in the fabric where the fringe is desired. Spray-starch the fabric if necessary.

2 Open the fabric, right side up. Using the creased line as a guide, sew a row of thread fringe over the blade of the tailor tack or fringing foot.

3 Fold back the hem along the crease, revealing the looped fringe along the edge. Press.

4. Change to the machine settings for Step Two. Place a layer of tear-away stabilizer underneath the wrong side of the hem. Select and sew a decorative stitch close to the fringe, securing the stitches in place. Carefully remove the stabilizer and trim away the hem allowance from the wrong side.

HANDLOOMS

Wide, elegant bands of beautifully embroidered motifs are an important addition to fine heirloom sewing. However, sewers quickly discover that the larger and more intricately embroidered the design, the greater the cost of the pre-made trim. Study the individual elements in an admired trim, then explore your sewing machine's decorative stitches to duplicate and create even more beautiful bands. Take advantage of machine memory capabilities to program multiple stitches together and sew repetitive patterns with ease.

MACHINE SET-UP

- **Stitch:** Any combination of decorative patterns
- **Presser Foot:** Open embroidery foot
- **Needles:** Universal needle, size #60 or #70
- **Threads:** Needle — Rayon or cotton embroidery
  Bobbin — 60 wt. cotton embroidery
- **Tension:** Normal to slightly loosened needle
- **Optional:** Engage needle down function

FABRIC CHOICES:

Batiste, lightweight linen, or pre-cut embroidery band yardage

ADDITIONAL SUPPLIES:

- Chalk or fabric marker
- Iron-on, removable stabilizer, fabric spray starch, or brush-on stabilizer

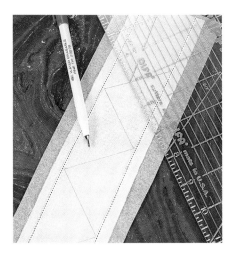

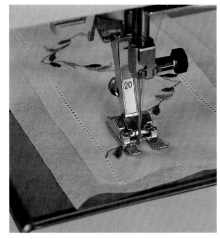

1 Cut the fabric yardage into the strip size desired, adding ¼" seam allowances on either side. Heavily stabilize the fabric strip with spray starch or liquid stabilizer. Using a fabric marking tool, mark the sewing guidelines.

2 Embroider the base embroidery. Using your stitch of choice, change the thread color as desired.

3 Add the larger size details, such as flowers, or bows. Add any smaller size details, such as small dots, in the final stitching.

4 Remove the stabilizer and press the finished handloom band.

Tip The most decorative designs on handloom bands are sewn in multiple layers. Review the desired design to determine the order in which you should sew.

HEIRLOOM SEWING, ENTREDEUX TO FLAT FABRIC

Another traditional favorite in heirloom sewing is sewing entredeux between rows of Swiss embroidered insertions or to flat fabric. These applications can be found in many places throughout the body of a garment. The technique is a simple two-step process.

MACHINE SET-UP

- **Stitch:** Step One: Straight, L — 2
  Step Two: Zig zag, L — $\frac{1}{2}$–1, W — $2\frac{1}{2}$
- **Presser Foot:** Step One: Edgestitch foot
  Step Two: Non-automatic buttonhole foot
  (a foot with narrow grooves on the bottom) or
  all-purpose foot
- **Needles:** Universal needle, size #60 or #70
- **Threads:** Needle and bobbin — 60 wt. cotton
  embroidery
- **Tension:** Normal
- **Optional:** Engage needle down function; adjust
  needle position

FABRIC CHOICES:

Traditional heirloom-quality handlooms, batiste, and entredeux

ADDITIONAL SUPPLIES:

- Spray starch

1 Lightly spray-starch and iron the entredeux and flat fabric edge or Swiss embroidery to be sewn.

2 With right sides together, position the entredeux on top of the flat fabric. Place the blade of the edgestitch foot close to the embroidered, outer edge of the entredeux. Adjust your needle position if necessary. Sew together using a straight stitch.

3 Trim the seam allowances to a slight ¼" on both fabrics.

continued

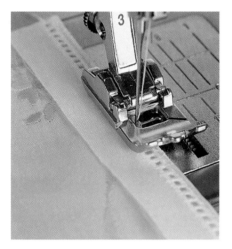

4 Reset the sewing machine for a zig zag stitch, replacing the edgestitch foot with the non-automatic buttonhole or all-purpose foot. Adjust the stitch to a wide, short zig zag. The left swing of the needle should fall close to the straight stitches. The right swing will fall over the cut edges of the entredeux and flat fabric. As the needle swings again to the left, the seam allowances will roll and be pulled into a clean edge.

5 Press the rolled seam toward the flat fabric or embroidery.

Tip This heirloom seaming technique is called a "rolled and whipped" seam.

HEIRLOOM SEWING, ENTREDEUX TO GATHERED LACES

Attaching a band of delicate entredeux to a gathered lace is a more advanced heirloom technique. Requiring patience and sewing at a slower speed, the beautiful results make the extra effort worthwhile. Duplicating vintage hand applications, a simple machine zig zag is the stitch of choice.

MACHINE SET-UP

- ♦ **Stitch:** Zig zag, L — 1½, W — 2–2½
- ♦ **Presser Foot:** Non-automatic buttonhole foot (a foot with narrow grooves on the bottom)
- ♦ **Needles:** Universal needle, size #70
- ♦ **Threads:** Needle and bobbin — 60 wt. cotton embroidery
- ♦ **Tension:** Normal
- ♦ **Optional:** Engage needle down function; adjust needle position

FABRIC CHOICES:

Traditional heirloom-quality edging laces and entredeux

ADDITIONAL SUPPLIES:

- ♦ Spray starch
- ♦ Air- or water-soluble fabric marker
- ♦ Embroidery scissors

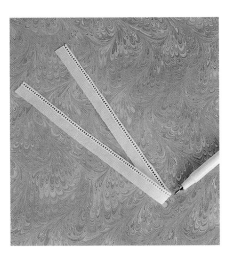

1 Lightly spray-starch and iron-dry the edging laces and entre-deux to be joined. Carefully trim away the batiste edge on one side of the entredeux. Fold and mark the center point of the entredeux and the flat edging lace band.

2 Using a pin, separate the threads found in the straight head-er of the edging lace. Gently pull on one of the heavier threads to gather the lace.

3 Match the marks and pin the beginning and center points of both the entredeux and gathered lace edging.

continued

4 Position and butt the entre-deux and gathered lace together so that the bulk of the seam will pass under the tunnel found on the bottom of the foot. Adjust your needle position right or left for correct sewing. Begin to slowly zig zag the trims together. One swing of the zig zag should fall into the holes woven into the entredeux strip, the other into the gathered header on the lace edging. Use the tip of a pin or seam ripper to adjust the gathers as you sew the seam.

HEIRLOOM SEWING, FLAT LACE TO ENTREDEUX

Multiple bands of delicate laces are often found with a sturdy embroidered band of eyelet holes inserted between them. This embroidered band, called entredeux, can be purchased pre-made, or can be duplicated on your sewing machine following the instructions for "Entredeux, Basic" and "Entredeux Corded". The lace and entredeux band are joined by using a simple zig zag stitch.

MACHINE SET-UP

- ♦ **Stitch:** Zig zag, L — approximately 1, W — 2½
- ♦ **Presser Foot:** Edgestitch foot
- ♦ **Needles:** Universal needle, size #60 or #70
- ♦ **Threads:** Needle and bobbin — 60 wt. cotton embroidery
- ♦ **Tension:** Normal
- ♦ **Optional:** Engage needle down function

FABRIC CHOICES:

Traditional heirloom-quality laces and entredeux

ADDITIONAL SUPPLIES:

- ♦ Spray starch
- ♦ Embroidery scissors

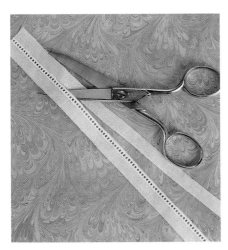

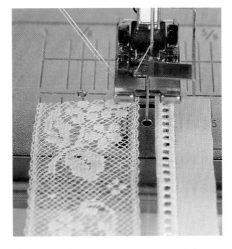

1 Spray-starch and press dry all laces and entredeux bands to be sewn. Trim away the batiste edge from one side of the entredeux, very close to the embroidery.

2 Butt the trimmed edge of the entredeux and the straight edge of the lace on either side of the center blade of the edgestitch foot.

3 Slowly begin to zig zag the pieces together, fine-tuning the width of the zig zag so the swing of the needle falls into the holes embroidered on the entredeux band and into the lace header.

continued

4 Press smooth when the stitch-ing is completed.

HEIRLOOM SEWING, LACE TO LACE

A traditional mainstay technique in heirloom sewing is the method of joining narrow, straight-edged bands of lace together to form wider pieces. These pieces may be used to finish the edge of a skirt or decorate the front of a blouse or dress. A simple zig zag stitch and an edgestitch foot, to help guide the laces, are all that is needed to complete your project.

MACHINE SET-UP

- ♦ **Stitch:** Zig zag, L —1, W — 2
- ♦ **Presser Foot:** Edgestitch foot
- ♦ **Needles:** Universal needle, size #60 or #70
- ♦ **Threads:** Needle and bobbin — 60 wt. cotton embroidery
- ♦ **Tension:** Normal
- ♦ **Optional:** Engage needle down function

FABRIC CHOICES:

Traditional heirloom-quality laces

ADDITIONAL SUPPLIES:

- ♦ Spray starch

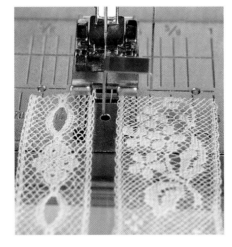

1 Lightly spray-starch and press dry all laces to be joined.

2 Position the straight edge of each piece of lace on the left and right sides of the center blade found on the edgestitch foot. The blade will act as a guide keeping the laces positioned correctly.

3 Begin to zig zag the laces together, allowing the left- and right-hand swing of the stitches to fall into the header of the laces.

continued

4 Press smooth when the stitching is completed.

HEIRLOOM SEWING, PUFFING

Puffing is an heirloom technique used to add visual interest and texture to a garment without the additional costs of fine laces and embroideries. Puffing strips can be sewn in straight rows in a garment, or even steamed and shaped into graceful hearts and scalloped edges.

MACHINE SET-UP

- ♦ **Stitch:** Straight, L — 2–4
- ♦ **Presser Foot:** Gathering foot
- ♦ **Needles:** Universal needle, size #60 or #70
- ♦ **Threads:** Needle and bobbin — 60 wt. cotton embroidery
- ♦ **Tension:** Normal to moderately tightened needle depending upon the weight of fabric selected
- ♦ **Optional:** Engage the basting function for extra fullness

FABRIC CHOICES:

Lightweight batiste

ADDITIONAL SUPPLIES:

- ♦ Spray starch

1 Tear, do not cut, the batiste strip for puffing. The width of the strip should be ½" wider on each side for the seam allowance; the length should be 2½–3 times the desired finished length. Lightly spray-starch and iron the batiste strip dry.

2 Insert one edge of the flat batiste strip under the gathering foot. Place the needle ½" in from the cut edge. Sew down one long side, creating soft gathers.

3 Turn over the batiste strip. Beginning at the same end as the first row of stitching, position the flat side of the batiste under the foot and gather the second side. (Note: It is important that you begin your gathering from the same end each time to avoid diagonal gathering.)

continued

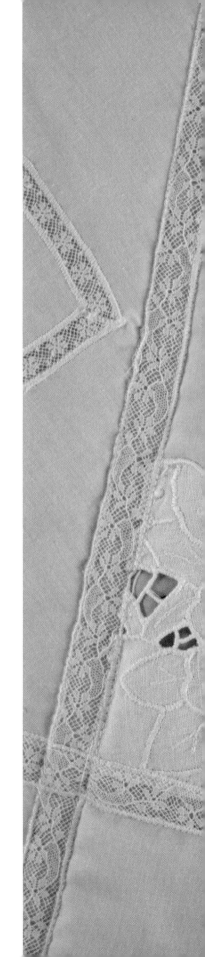

4 Gently pull on the right and left side of the gathered strip. The gathers will straighten and become more horizontal. Pin the puffing strip to an ironing surface, steam-press, and allow to dry in the pinned position. Attach the finished strip to lace, or entredeux as desired.

Tip Tearing the batiste strip will assure that the fabric is on grain, essential for straight, even puffing.

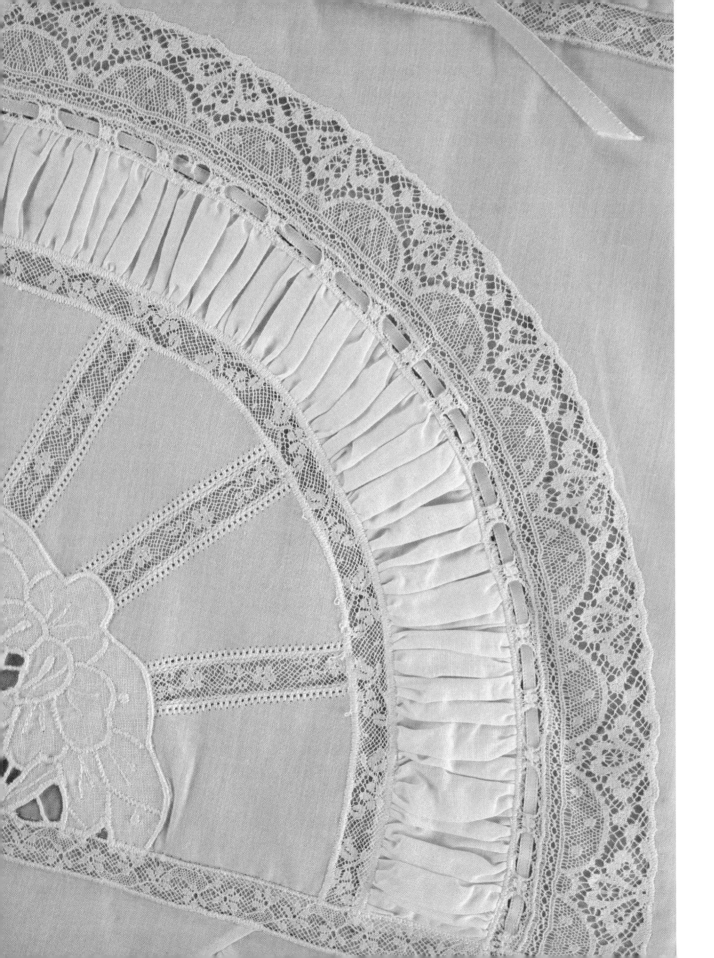

HEMSTITCHING, DOUBLE WING NEEDLE

Hemstitching using a double wing needle can create beautiful and more dramatic results than with a single wing needle. Characterized by two needles on one shank, a double wing needle will have one wing and one universal needle. Very simple stitch patterns sewn with this specialized needle create elegant effects.

MACHINE SET-UP

- ♦ **Stitch:** Straight, L — approximately 2
- ♦ **Presser Foot:** Any clear embroidery or traditional buttonhole foot
- ♦ **Needles:** Double wing needle, size #100
- ♦ **Threads:** Needle and bobbin — 60 wt. cotton or rayon embroidery
- ♦ **Tension:** Normal to slightly tightened needle
- ♦ **Optional:** Engage needle down function

FABRIC CHOICES:

Light- to medium weight woven fabrics, natural fibers preferred, such as linen, batiste, and organdy

ADDITIONAL SUPPLIES:

- ♦ Air- or water-soluble fabric marker
- ♦ Spray starch
- ♦ Lightweight tear-away stabilizer

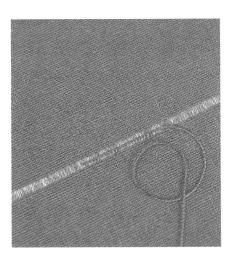

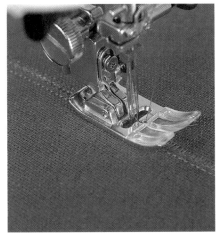

1 Remove several fiber threads from the area to be stitched to give a more defined look to the holes created by the wing needle. Prepare the fabric in the same manner as "Hemstitching, Single Wing Needle".

2 Sew down the center of the guideline for the first row of stitches. Guide the needles so that the left wing needle sews into the void created by the pulled threads. The other universal needle should sew on the cross woven fibers.

3 Raise the needles and presser foot, and turn the fabric to sew in the opposite direction. At a reduced speed, sew the second row of straight stitches, positioning the fabric so the wing needle sews again in the hole created by the first row of stitching.

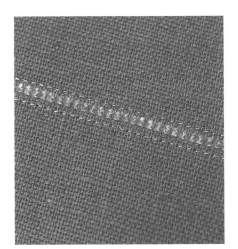

4 Remove the tear-away stabilizer and press.

HEMSTITCHING, SINGLE WING NEEDLE

Hemstitching is an embellishment detail that adds an understated and classic accent to any sewing project. Originally sewn by specialty hemstitching machines in the early 1900's, home sewers can now duplicate this subtle detail by using a single or double wing needle. Hemstitching details can be found decorating the collars and cuffs of fine blouses, dresses, and nightwear, or used as an upscale hem finish on linen table runners and napkins. The configuration of the stitches selected for hemstitching need to sew in and out of the same hole a number of times, literally creating tiny "holes" in the fabric with the wing needle.

MACHINE SET-UP

- **Stitch:** Zig zag, pin or daisy/star stitch, L and W — approximately 2
- **Presser Foot:** Clear embroidery foot or non-automatic buttonhole foot (a foot with narrow grooves on the bottom)
- **Needles:** Single wing needle, size #100 or #110
- **Threads:** Needle — 60 wt. cotton embroidery or 50 wt. silk
  Bobbin — 60 wt. cotton embroidery
- **Tension:** Normal
- **Optional:** Engage needle down function and any width limitation function; adjust stitch balance if necessary

FABRIC CHOICES:

Light- to medium weight woven natural fibers such as, linen, organdy or batiste

ADDITIONAL SUPPLIES:

- Air- or water-soluble fabric or chalk marker
- Spray starch
- Optional: Single layer of lightweight tear-away stabilizer

1 Spray the fabric with starch; iron dry. Repeat this procedure a number of times to create a very crisp fabric. Using a fabric marker, draw in a stitching guideline. Place a single layer of lightweight tear-away stabilizer underneath the area to be stitched if desired.

2 Select your stitch pattern and sew the first row. With the needle in the left swing of the stitch, turn the fabric to sew in the opposite direction. Sew the second row at a slower speed. The left swing of the stitch should fall into the left holes of the first row of stitching.

3 Remove the tear-away stabilizer and press when the rows of stitching are completed.

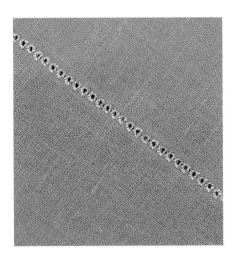

4 If you have selected the daisy or star stitch, sew a single row on the drawn line.

5 Due to the multiple forward and backward motion of the stitch design, it may be necessary to adjust the balance of your stitch to make sure that the needle falls into the same center part of the stitch each time.

LACEMAKING, DECORATIVE STITCH

Elegant lace can be made utilizing the many decorative stitches found on your sewing machine and cotton netting. Duplicate more expensive laces quickly and easily. An alternative to single needle lacemaking is using a double needle on sheer fabrics. Try one technique or both on your next heirloom project.

MACHINE SET-UP

♦ **Stitch:** Decorative stitch of choice, L and W — Preset
♦ **Presser Foot:** Open or clear embroidery foot
♦ **Needles:** Universal needle, size #70
♦ **Threads:** Needle and bobbin — 40 wt. or 60 wt. cotton or rayon embroidery
♦ **Tension:** Slightly loosened needle

FABRIC CHOICES:

Cotton netting or sheer fabrics such as organdy or organza

ADDITIONAL SUPPLIES:

♦ Water-soluble stabilizer
♦ Spray starch
♦ Spring-loaded or wooden embroidery hoop
♦ Optional: Double needle, size #2.0/80

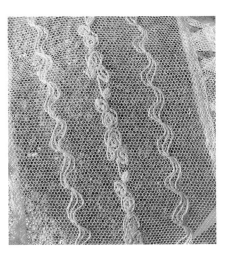

1 Thread your machine with the cotton or rayon thread. Starch the cotton netting and press dry. Layer the cotton netting between two pieces of water-soluble stabilizer and place in a hoop.

2 Select your favorite embroidery stitch and begin stitching. Use your presser foot as your guide to keep the rows of stitching straight and even.

3 When you are done stitching, rinse away the water-soluble stabilizer and press dry.

continued

153

4 If you are using the newly created lace as an insertion, spray-starch the piece again prior to stitching into your garment.

5 Another lacemaking technique utilizes a double needle. Stabilize your sheer fabric as above. Following the instructions for "Stippling, Basic", carefully swirl your stitches across your fabric.

LACEMAKING, FREE-MOTION

Lacemaking is an elegant free-motion stitching technique that uses cotton netting and fine threads. Create your own lace edgings or insertions using this method. This delicate technique requires the same machine control that free-motion embroidery does but the designs are not filled in so solidly. Airy and light, lacemaking adds the final professional touch to any garment.

MACHINE SET-UP

- ◆ **Stitch:** Step One: Straight
  Step Two: Zig zag, W — 2–5 based on the size of the design
- ◆ **Presser Foot:** Darning or free-motion embroidery foot
- ◆ **Needles:** Universal needle, size #60 or #70
- ◆ **Threads:** Needle — 40 wt. or 60 wt. cotton or rayon embroidery
  Bobbin — 60 wt. cotton embroidery
- ◆ **Tension:** Normal to slightly loosened needle
- ◆ **Feed Dogs:** Lowered
- ◆ **Optional:** Engage needle down function or adjust presser foot pressure for free-motion work

FABRIC CHOICES:

Cotton netting as embroidery base
Linen, silk, or other firm fabrics to attach finished lace

ADDITIONAL SUPPLIES:

- ◆ Water-soluble stabilizer
- ◆ Air- or water-soluble fabric marker
- ◆ Spring-loaded or wooden embroidery hoop
- ◆ Embroidery or applique scissors

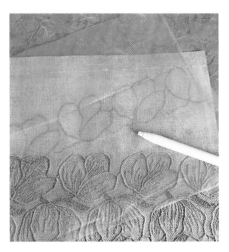

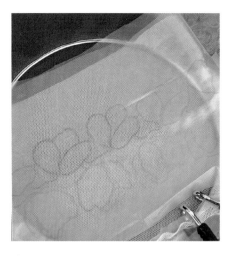

1 Transfer your design to one layer of water-soluble stabilizer using your marking pen.

2 Cut your netting the width of the project including any seam allowances.

3 Layer your fabrics and stabilizer from the bottom up in the following manner: one to two layers of water-soluble stabilizer, firm fabric, cotton netting half overlapping the firm fabric, and one to two layers of stabilizer with the traced design on top. Insert all the layers into the embroidery hoop centering the design.

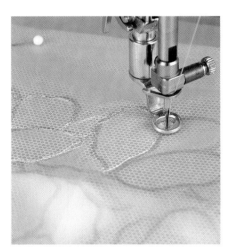

4 Following the settings for Step One, outline the design with the straight stitch. Repeat the straight stitching a second time to secure the following zig zag stitches.

5 Adjust your machine to Step Two settings, and oversew the securing stitches with your zig zag along the upper edge connecting the netting to the firm fabric.

continued

6 Carefully trim the firm fabric from around the design on the back. Place a layer of water-soluble stabilizer under the netting before continuing.

7 Complete the zig zag stitching around the design on the stabilized netting only.

8 Trim away the netting from the bottom edge. Remove the stabilizer and press the finished lace.

Tip To achieve smooth, contour zig zag stitching, only move the hoop in a back and forth or left and right motion. Try not to rotate the hoop at all.

MONOGRAMMING, FREE-MOTION

Similar to free-motion embroidery, free-motion monogramming allows you the freedom to create your own script style and design. Many sewing machines, today, have built-in monogramming features but you are still limited to the sizes available on your machine. Combine built-in stitches with your own free-motion designs for one-of-a-kind personalized detailing.

MACHINE SET-UP

- **Stitch:** Zig zag, L — ½, W — 3½
- **Presser Foot:** Darning or free-motion foot
- **Needles:** Universal needle, size #80
- **Threads:** Needle — 30 wt., 40 wt., or 50 wt. cotton or rayon embroidery, metallic
  Bobbin — 60 wt. cotton embroidery
- **Tension:** Loosen needle
- **Feed Dogs:** Lowered
- **Optional:** Engage needle down function or adjust presser foot pressure for free-motion work

FABRIC CHOICES:

As desired

ADDITIONAL SUPPLIES:

- Tear-away stabilizer
- Spring-loaded or wooden embroidery hoop
- Air- or water-soluble fabric marker

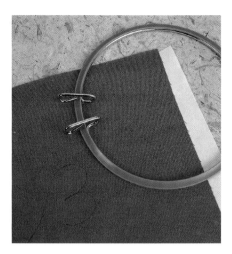

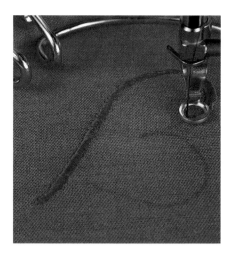

1 Layer your fabric over the tear-away stabilizer. Trace your letter(s) on the fabric with the marking pen. Insert the layers into the embroidery hoop. (Note: Following a marked design is a beneficial guide for a beginner.)

2 Lower the feed dogs and, with your hands on each side of the hoop, begin sewing keeping the zig zag stitches horizontal. Only move the hoop right or left or up and down; do not twist the hoop. The stitching will take on a thick and thin appearance as you move around the letter(s).

Tip For a beginner, it is helpful to sketch out your design prior to stitching so you can see how it will look. It's always best to practice on scrap fabric before beginning your final project.

MONOGRAMMING, SATIN STITCH

Satin stitch or block monogramming is a very easy method of personalizing all your work. Generally, straight lines are used rather than curves and swirls to create the letters. For a more raised effect, a cord can be added and satin-stitched over. Try this simple technique as your first experience with monogramming.

MACHINE SET-UP

- ♦ **Stitch:** Zig zag, L — ½, W — 3–3½
- ♦ **Presser Foot:** Open or clear embroidery foot, cording foot
- ♦ **Needles:** Match to fabric
- ♦ **Threads:** Needle — 30 wt., 40 wt., or 50 wt. cotton or rayon embroidery, metallic
  Bobbin — 60 wt. cotton embroidery
  Filler — Gimp or topstitching thread
- ♦ **Tension:** Loosen needle
- ♦ **Optional:** Engage needle down function

FABRIC CHOICES:

As desired

ADDITIONAL SUPPLIES:

- ♦ Tear-away stabilizer
- ♦ Air- or water-soluble fabric marker
- ♦ Spring-loaded or wooden embroidery hoop

1 Mark the fabric with your marking pen. Layer the fabric over the tear-away stabilizer and insert the layers into the hoop.

2 Beginning in one corner, stitch down one side. At the corner stop with the needle lowered on the outside edge.

3 Pivot and stitch down the next side oversewing the corner. Stop at the corner with the needle down on the outside edge. Pivot. Repeat this procedure around the entire letter.

continued

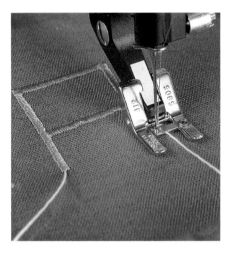

4. For a raised effect, thread the gimp cord through the hole or guide on the foot. Satin-stitch down the side as above. At corners, carefully pivot keeping the gimp under the foot and continue satin-stitching as above.

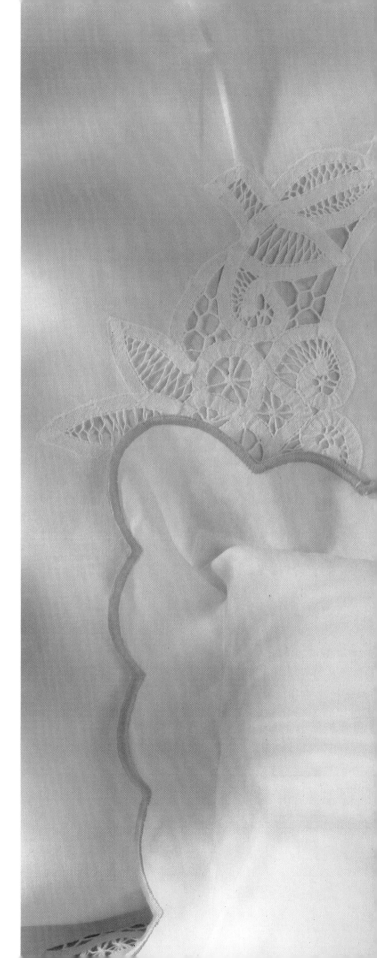

MULTI-NEEDLE TECHNIQUES

A simple way to enrich the look of straight or decorative stitching is to use a double or triple needle. Once the needle is inserted and the machine is set up, the stitching is sewn in the usual way, but the look is very different. Often used for decorative work, there are also practical applications, such as a hem that "gives", which is suitable for knit fabrics.

Double or twin needles are available in various sizes. The point size is the same as other universal needles (#60–110); however, there is also the width between the two needles to be considered. Printed on the package in millimeters, the needles are available in 1.6, 2.0, 2.5, 3.0, 4.0, 6.0, and 8.0mm widths. The wider the distance between needles, the more limiting the stitch choices will be. The wider 6.0mm and the 8.0mm needles may not work with all sewing machines. Most machines have a maximum stitch width of 5mm, therefore the double needle needs to be less than that width. Also available is a size #3.0/75 double needle with a stretch point for use on knits.

Similar to a double needle, the triple needle is available in size #3.0/80. In this case, the 3.0 refers to the distance between the two outer needles. This needle works best with a straight stitch or a very narrow stitch width. Mix two or three colors to create interesting looks or match all three spools to the fabric for a subtle tone-on-tone effect. The three lines of stitching add texture and dimension to the fabric.

MACHINE SET-UP

- ◆ **Stitch:** Of choice, L — as desired, W — within the maximum stitch width
- ◆ **Presser Foot:** Appropriate to the stitch
- ◆ **Needles:** Double or triple needle, size matched to fabric
- ◆ **Threads:** Needle — All-purpose polyester; cotton or rayon embroidery thread (2 or 3 spools)
    Bobbin — 60 wt. cotton embroidery
- ◆ **Tension:** Normal

FABRIC CHOICES:

As desired

ADDITIONAL SUPPLIES:

- ◆ Appropriate stabilizer if necessary
- ◆ Empty bobbin

1 If using either a double or triple needle, set the width of the stitch so the needles will not hit the foot as the stitch is formed. To determine the maximum width allowed, subtract the width of the needles from the maximum width of the sewing machine. Sew at a controlled moderate speed.

continued

167

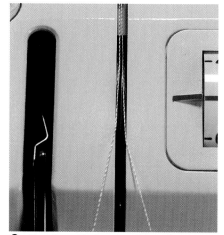

2 To thread the machine for a double needle, place one thread on each side of the tension disc and bypass the last thread guide before the needle with one of the threads. This will help to keep the threads separate, eliminating tangling. For a triple needle, place two threads on one side of the tension disc and one on the other.

3 Depending on the weight of the fabric, interface or stabilize the fabric as needed before stitching. Mark the positioning for the desired pattern on the fabric. If stitching a linear design, mark the first line and use the quilting bar and/or the presser foot for easy guiding on the fabric.

4 When removing the fabric from under the double or triple needle, once stitching is completed, hold the needle and bobbin threads at the end of the stitching to avoid puckering the stitches.

Tip Most sewing machines are not equipped with three spool pins. When working with a triple needle, a good method of extending one of the spool pins is to slip a plastic drinking straw over it and place a full bobbin and one spool of thread on the straw. Place the second spool of thread on the second spool pin. Continue threading as directed above.

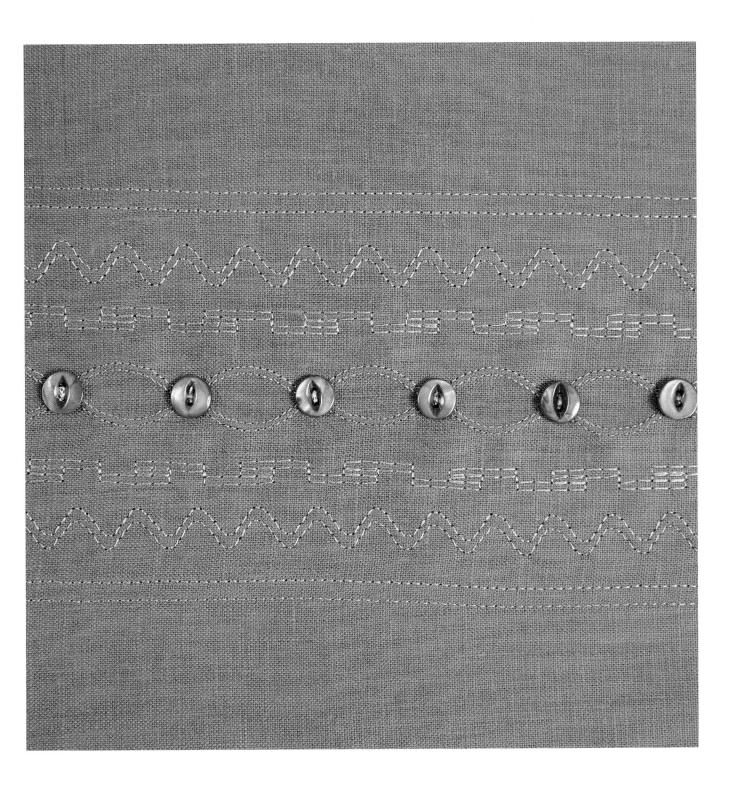

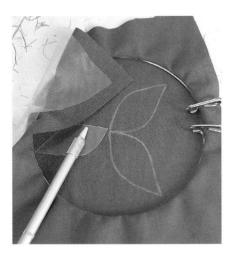

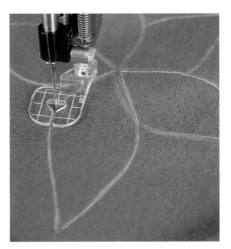

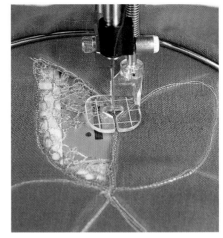

1 Layer the water-soluble stabilizer under the base fabric and place in the hoop. Trace the design on the fabric.

2 Lower your feed dogs and stitch around the design following the lines. For extra stability, stitch a second time. Cut away the fabric only inside the stitching lines.

3 Using a circular motion, begin stitching in one corner and swirl your stitches on and off the fabric. Fill in the entire area with swirling stitches trying to keep the stitching motion even and smooth.

4 Cover the edges with a smooth free-motion satin stitch. Remove the piece from the hoop and carefully wash away the stabilizer from the open areas. Press flat between a Teflon™ press cloth.

Tip When removing the water-soluble stabilizer, hold the piece under the water with the stabilizer on the bottom. Let the water gently flow through the stitched area and not onto the rest of the fabric. This helps keep the water-soluble stabilizer from running back into the fabric.

PASSEMENTERIE

Passementerie is a technique of applying narrow tapes or trims in decorative designs across the fabric. The tape is stitched down using a straight stitch and formed into curves, zig zags, or other designs. Purchased soutache is the perfect trim to use for this technique as it forms into designs relatively easily.

MACHINE SET-UP

- **Stitch:** Straight, L — 1½–2
- **Presser Foot:** Braiding foot
- **Needles:** Universal needle, size #80
- **Threads:** Needle and bobbin — All-purpose polyester, match color to soutache braid
- **Tension:** Normal
- **Optional:** Engage needle down function

FABRIC CHOICES:

Stable fabrics such as linen, wool, heavier cottons

ADDITIONAL SUPPLIES:

- Soutache braid trim
- Fusible knit interfacing
- Chalk or fabric marker
- Optional: Tear-away stabilizer

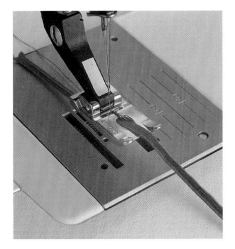

1 Apply the fusible knit interfacing to the wrong side of the base fabric. It will provide stability for the trim.

2 Thread the trim through the hole on the front and under the back of the braiding foot.

3 Mark your design on the fabric with the chalk marker. Begin by stitching straight lines to learn to control the feeding of the soutache through the foot. The stitches will fall into the groove on the trim.

continued

4 To stitch a zig zag design, stop with the needle down at the point. Raise the foot, pivot, and flip the soutache. Make sure the soutache is flat and that your next stitch will catch the trim. Continue stitching. Repeat at each point.

5 For curves, stitch very slowly, pivoting often. Make sure the soutache remains flat. (Note: If the soutache is pulled too tightly around the curve, the fabric will pull in and not lie flat.)

Tip Add additional tear-away stabilizer to any area with complicated designs. It will help the fabric from puckering.

PINTUCKS, CORDED

Sewing pintucks using a coordinating or contrasting color filler cord affords the sewer numerous creative opportunities as well as providing stability to the pintuck being sewn. Using a matching filler cord creates a pronounced, raised pintuck; switching to a pastel or brightly colored filler cord adds a shadow effect, producing a raised tuck with a subtle hint of color. Sewing pintucks with a filler cord adds to the integrity of the tuck. The pintuck is less likely to be drawn off grain when sewing on a single layer of fabric and cannot be pressed flat with a heavy hand at the iron. Making corded pintucks is an easily learned technique, quickly mastered by sewers of all skill levels.

MACHINE SET-UP

♦ **Stitch:** Straight, L — 2½
♦ **Presser Foot:** 3 to 7 groove pintuck feet
♦ **Needles:** Double needle, size #2.0/80 – #8.0/80
♦ **Threads:** Needle — 2 spools of matching thread, cotton or rayon embroidery or all-purpose polyester
   Bobbin — All-purpose polyester
   Filler — Heavier threads or cords, such as, Cordonnet topstitching thread, perle cotton #3 or #5, baby yarn
♦ **Tension:** Normal

FABRIC CHOICES:

A single layer of any type fabric provides the best results. Select batistes, silks, and blouse-weight linens for heirloom garments. However, lightweight woolens can also be pintucked using wider twin needles and heavier or multiple filler cords.

ADDITIONAL SUPPLIES:

♦ Air- or water-soluble fabric marker
♦ Dental floss threader

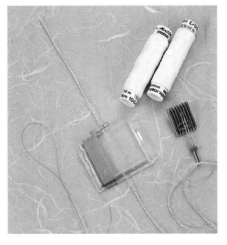

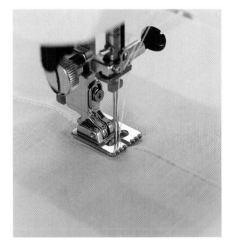

1 Establish the straight of grain on the fabric by pulling a cross-wise thread. Mark this line with the fabric marker to better see while stitching.

2 Attach the appropriate needle plate to hold the filler cord or insert the filler cord up through or under the needle plate following the instructions with your machine. Install the desired size twin needle and corresponding pintuck foot. Leave a 6" tail of filler cord behind the foot.

3 Center the middle groove of the pintuck foot over the marked grainline. Begin to sew the first pintuck at a slow, even speed. The filler cord will automatically be caught in the bobbin stitches.

continued

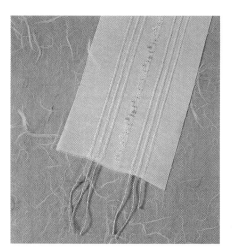

4 Continue to sew additional tucks, using the grooves located on the underside of the foot to guide straight, evenly spaced pin-tucks.

Tip When stitching shadow tucks, the more densely woven the fabric, the more brightly colored the filler cord should be. Experiment with a variety of shades to test color shadowing before beginning your project.

QUILTING, HAND-LOOK

This unusual technique offers the look of a hand-sewn running stitch using cotton embroidery thread in the bobbin, monofilament thread in the needle, and a simple feather stitch. The needle tension is adjusted so the bobbin thread pulls to the surface of the fabric alternating with the monofilament. The spacing of the two gives the illusion of large stitches moving across the fabric. Some sewing machine models have this as a built-in stitch pattern. Use this stitch anywhere a pronounced straight stitch or the look of hand quilting is desired. This technique works best with low-loft cotton battings.

MACHINE SET-UP

♦ **Stitch:** Feather stitch, L — 4–5; W — 0
♦ **Presser Foot:** All-purpose, jeans, or walking foot
♦ **Needles:** Universal needle, size #80 or #90 depending upon depth of fabric layers
♦ **Threads:** Needle — Monofilament
  Bobbin — 30 wt. cotton embroidery
♦ **Tension:** Tighten needle tension to 7 or above
♦ **Optional:** Adjust balance feature, if necessary, to make stitch more even

FABRIC CHOICES:

Quilting-weight cottons ideal

ADDITIONAL SUPPLIES:

♦ Water-soluble fabric marker
♦ Clear ruler

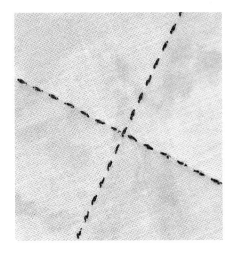

1 Using a water-soluble pen and clear ruler, draw in lines for quilting. Layer the pieced top, batting and backing, and position underneath the presser foot.

2 Slowly begin to sew on the marked lines. The forward and backward motion of the feather stitch will oversew itself, placing stitch on top of stitch.

3 This motion, coupled with the increased needle tension, will draw up the bobbin thread condensing it into a traditional, hand-picked-looking running stitch.

Tips Sew at a slow, even speed for best results. Make sure the monofilament spool feeds smoothly while sewing. Take a couple of preliminary stitches to fully secure the monofilament thread into the fabric. Begin your row of quilting stitches in a discreet part of your project to avoid any irregular appearing patterns.

QUILT-PIECING METHODS, EASY TRIANGLES

Accurate, even triangles can be stitched quickly on the sewing machine. Using this method, two pairs of triangles are sewn at one time. As with all piecing methods, accurate cutting is vital to the success of the technique.

MACHINE SET-UP

- **Stitch:** Straight
- **Presser Foot:** All-purpose foot
- **Needles:** Universal needle, size #80
- **Threads:** Needle and bobbin — All-purpose polyester
- **Tension:** Normal

FABRIC CHOICES:

Cotton fabrics, prints and solids

ADDITIONAL SUPPLIES:

- Rotary cutter and mat
- Clear ruler
- Air- or water-soluble fabric marker

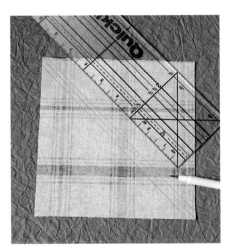

1 Cut two squares, the size based on the final triangle size plus ¼" seam allowances. Using your clear ruler and fabric marker, draw one line diagonally from one corner to the other on one square. Measure ¼" away from the drawn line on each side and draw two more lines. (Note: The outer lines are the stitching lines and the center line is the cutting line.)

2 Pin the two squares together. Following the drawn lines, stitch on the outer lines.

3 Using the center line as a guide, cut through both layers along the mark.

continued

4 Press the seams open. Four triangles have now been easily and quickly sewn together.

QUILT-PIECING METHODS, SEMINOLE PATCHWORK

This exciting and colorful piecing or patchwork technique is derived from methods introduced by the Seminole Indian women of the Florida Everglades. Designs created in bright, solid-colored fabrics look more difficult than they actually are to sew. Simply, the basic technique involves sewing strips of fabric together, cutting the strips into pieces and then sewing the pieces back together again. Many unique and exciting variations are possible.

MACHINE SET-UP

- **Stitch:** Straight, L — 2–2½
- **Presser Foot:** ¼" foot
- **Needles:** Universal needle, size #80
- **Threads:** Needle and bobbin — All-purpose polyester
- **Tension:** Normal

FABRIC CHOICES:

Solid-colored cotton fabrics

ADDITIONAL SUPPLIES:

- Rotary cutter and mat
- Clear ruler
- Air- or water-soluble fabric marker

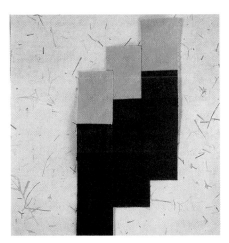

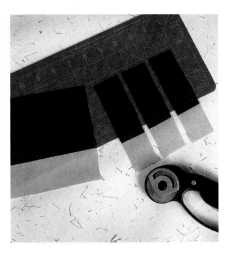

1 For basic Seminole patchwork, cut strips of fabric of varying widths. As a beginner, start with just three different colored strips.

2 Using your ¼" foot and with right sides together, stitch the strips along the long edges. Press the seams to one side.

3 With your ruler and marking pen, mark the sewn pieces at 2" intervals along one long edge. Using the rotary cutter, mat, and ruler, cut across the strips making a new three-colored piece.

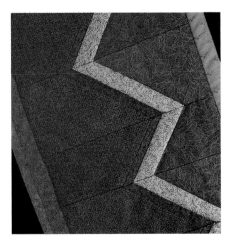

4 Again with right sides together, take two newly cut pieces and offset their alignment by one row. Pin. Stitch the seams using the ¼" foot. Press seams to one side.

5 Once all cut pieces are sewn together again, from the right side, place the ruler along the upper inner corner raw edge and draw a line. Repeat this procedure along the bottom inner raw edge. Use this marking as your stitching line for applying bands or other rows of piecing.

6 Another method of piecing involves marking and cutting angle pieces. Follow Steps 1 and 2 to begin this method.

continued

7 For 2" strips, use your clear ruler and first measure from the bottom corner over 3" along one long edge. From that point, measure in 2" increments across this long edge. From the same end of the strip, measure in 2" increments from the top corner. Connect the marks and cut along the diagonal marks.

8 With rights sides together, offset the alignment of the pieces and stitch using the ¼" foot. Following Step 5, mark the newly sewn strip in the same manner.

9 Experiment with cutting and piecing your sewn strips in a variety of configurations.

Tip When pressing patchwork, it is best to press the seam toward the darker fabric.

QUILT-PIECING METHODS, STRIP

Piecing is the basis for most quilt-design projects. Squares, strips, or triangles are the most common shapes used for piecing. Sewn together in a variety of ways, beautiful designs are then created. Antique pieced patterns are easy to stitch on the sewing machine.

MACHINE SET-UP

- ◆ **Stitch:** Straight
- ◆ **Presser Foot:** ¼″ foot
- ◆ **Needles:** Universal needle, size #80
- ◆ **Threads:** Needle and bobbin — All-purpose polyester
- ◆ **Tension:** Normal
- ◆ **Optional:** Engage needle down function

FABRIC CHOICES:

Cotton fabrics, prints or solids

ADDITIONAL SUPPLIES:

- ◆ Rotary cutter and mat
- ◆ Clear ruler

1 Using your rotary cutter, mat, and ruler, cut squares or strips of fabric allowing for a ¼" seam allowance on all sides.

2 With right sides together, place two squares under the ¼" foot. Begin stitching at the edge of the squares. Stitch the squares together completely.

3 To save time on proj-ects involving lots of piecing, butt the edges of the next two squares against the previously stitched squares. Clip the squares apart once all the pieces are joined together. Press all seams to one side preferably toward the darker fabric.

4 With right sides together, pin the stitched squares together with another set of stitched squares. Match the seams and make sure the pressed seam allowances are going in opposite directions to avoid undue bulk at the seams. Stitch using the ¼" foot.

Tip In piecing, it is very impor-tant that all the fabric sections be cut accurately. Accurate cutting assists in accurate stitching. As a result, points will meet precisely at the seams.

QUILT-PIECING METHODS, VICTORIAN

Victorian patchwork adds a new dimension to the art of quilting. The crazy piecing method of using elegant scraps of fabric, no matter what size or shape, and decorative embroidery stitches is fun and creative. Try velvets, brocades, silks or men's old ties as your patchwork fabrics. Let your imagination take off and create your very own heirloom piece.

MACHINE SET-UP

♦ **Stitch:** Step One: Straight, L — 2–2½
    Step Two: Any decorative stitch
♦ **Presser Foot:** ¼" foot or walking foot
♦ **Needles:** Match to fabric
♦ **Threads:** Step One: Needle and bobbin — All-purpose polyester
    Step Two: Needle and bobbin — Cotton or rayon embroidery
♦ **Tension:** Normal

FABRIC CHOICES:

Silks, velvets, brocades, satins—any elegant fabric of choice

ADDITIONAL SUPPLIES:

♦ Fleece or muslin for backing
♦ Optional: Fusible knit interfacing

1 Select your fabrics, backing and pattern. Cut your pattern piece from the fleece or muslin to use as the backing. Stabilize your fabrics with the fusible tricot interfacing, if necessary.

2 With right side down and using your ¼" or walking foot, stitch the first piece of stabilized fabric to the backing along one edge wherever desired. Flip the piece back to the right side and press the seam down.

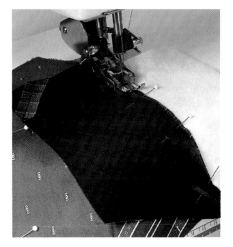

3 Again with right side down, place the next stabilized piece over the first, in a random manner, matching the raw edges along the unsewn edge. Stitch along this edge. Flip and press the seam down.

continued

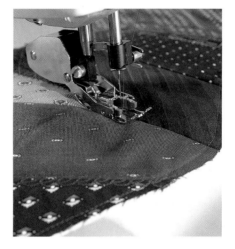

4 Continue stitching all the pieces down in a random manner across the entire pattern piece. Press flat. Use your pattern to trim any uneven edges.

5 Select a decorative stitch and thread your machine with a decorative thread. From the right side, stitch over a seam joining two sections, adding an interesting decorative detail.

Tip Most sewing machines today have a selection of built-in crazy quilt embroidery stitches, duplicating the beautiful hand stitches of the Victorian era.

QUILTING STYLES, ECHO

Echo quilting is a fun technique using a basic straight stitch to create concentric lines outside the pieced or appliqué design. This technique can be achieved either free-motion or with the use of the feed dogs. Space the distance between each line of quilting according to the size of the piece and the area to be quilted.

MACHINE SET-UP

- ◆ **Stitch:** Straight
- ◆ **Presser Foot:** Clear or open embroidery, darning or free-motion foot
- ◆ **Needles:** Match to fabric
- ◆ **Threads:** Needle and bobbin — All-purpose polyester or monofilament
- ◆ **Tension:** Normal
- ◆ **Feed Dogs:** Down if using darning or free-motion foot
- ◆ **Optional:** Engage needle down function

FABRIC CHOICES:

As desired

ADDITIONAL SUPPLIES:

- ◆ Batting of choice
- ◆ Quilt pins

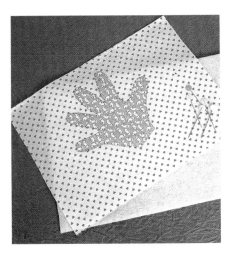  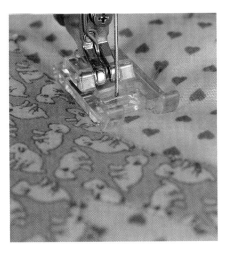

1 Layer your pieced or appliquéd fabric over the batting. Add backing according to the pattern or final project.

2 Pin the layers together at approximately 2" intervals to avoid shifting.

3 Using the edge of the presser foot as your guide, begin stitching around the edge of the design. (Note: If you are using a darning or free-motion foot, move and turn the fabric at an consistent speed to keep the stitches even.)

continued

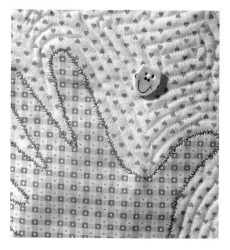

4 Continue around the design locking the stitches at the end. Move out one presser foot width and echo the first row of stitching. Repeat as often as desired.

Tip To create overall echo quilting on a wall hanging or quilt, outline each section in sequence. That is, stitch the first row around all areas, then begin again with the second row of stitching. Stitching lines will begin to intersect the farther out the echo lines get. To avoid stitching lines crossing each other, begin creating larger outlines.

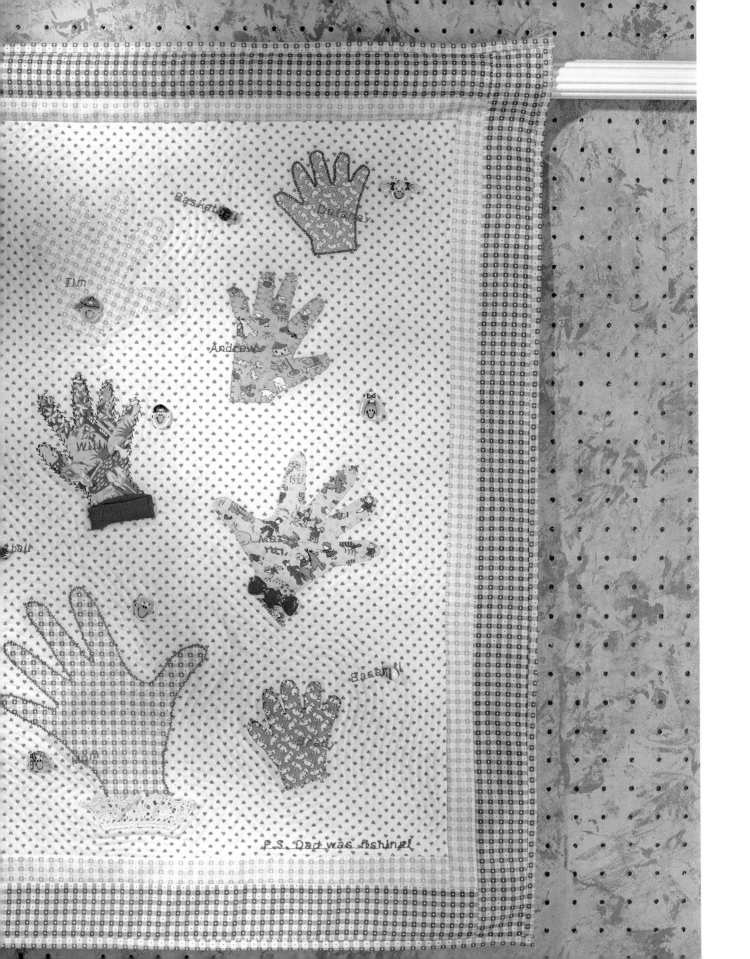

QUILTING STYLES, LINEAR

Linear or straight-line quilting is the easiest form of quilting to do for the home sewer. All that is needed is a walking foot and guide and a little innovation. These straight lines can take on many forms being stitched into channels, diamonds, squares, parallelograms, and more. Try a striped fabric as a "cheater" if you are just a beginning quilter.

MACHINE SET-UP

- ♦ **Stitch:** Straight
- ♦ **Presser Foot:** Walking foot and quilting guide
- ♦ **Needles:** Match to fabric
- ♦ **Threads:** Needle and bobbin — All-purpose polyester
- ♦ **Tension:** Normal
- ♦ **Optional:** Engage needle down function

FABRIC CHOICES:

As desired
Cotton muslin for backing

ADDITIONAL SUPPLIES:

- ♦ Quilt pins
- ♦ Batting or thermal fleece

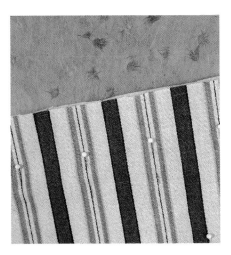

1 Layer your fabric over the batting or fleece. Pin at approximately 2" intervals. (Note: You may want to sandwich the batting between the outer fabric and a piece of muslin for a smoother feed. Smooth all layers before pinning.)

2 Using the stripes as your guide, stitch down each line producing a channel-quilted effect.

3 Attach the quilt guide at the distance desired, measuring from the needle. Begin stitching perpendicular to the previous rows of stitching creating a square or rectangular design.

continued

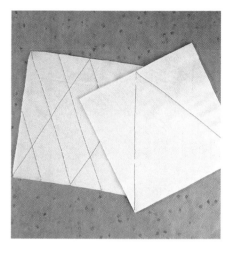

4 To stitch a parallelogram quilting effect, begin by first folding and pressing your fabric at a diagonal across the center of the piece. Use the crease as your guide for the first row of quilt stitching.

Tip Experiment with the various linear quilting designs based on your fabric choice.

5 Using your quilting guide set at the desired distance, stitch parallel rows moving out from the center line on each side. To achieve the diamond effect, fold and press the fabric in half. Stitch straight lines as above.

6 For a diamond design, begin by finding the center point of one side and mark. From that point, fold in one corner using the bottom opposite corner as the anchor point. Fold in the other corner in the same way. Again using the fold as your guide, stitch. You will have stitched large "V" on your fabric. Find the center on the opposite side and repeat the above procedure, creating diamonds.

QUILTING STYLES, OUTLINE

Outline quilting involves using the design printed or woven on the fabric and literally outlining it with thread. The area remains puffy with the other areas not as defined. The closer together the outline stitching, a flatter three-dimensional effect is achieved. A free-hand technique, outline quilting is perfect for pillows, comforters, and bedspreads.

MACHINE SET-UP

- ◆ **Stitch:** Straight
- ◆ **Presser Foot:** Darning or free-motion foot, free-motion quilting foot
- ◆ **Needles:** Match to fabric
- ◆ **Threads:** Needle — Monofilament
  Bobbin — 60 wt. cotton embroidery
- ◆ **Feed Dogs:** Down
- ◆ **Optional:** Engage needle down function

FABRIC CHOICES:

As desired, large prints best
Cotton muslin for backing

ADDITIONAL SUPPLIES:

- ◆ Puffy batting
- ◆ Quilt pins

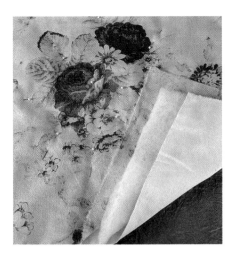 

1 Sandwich the batting between the outer fabric and cotton muslin. Pin at approximately 2" intervals to keep the layers from shifting.

2 With right sides up, use your design as your guide and outline stitch. Be sure to secure the monofilament thread at the beginning and the end.

Tip The closer together the stitching lines around and within the design, the less effective this technique becomes.

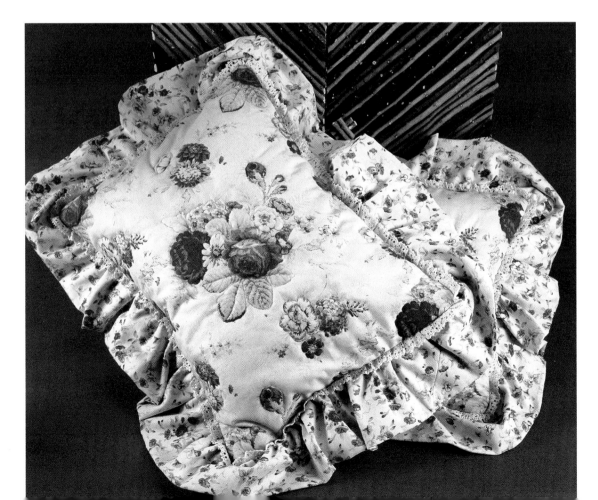

QUILTING STYLES, SASHIKO

Sashiko is quilting simplicity at its elegant best. This quilting/mending art form was originally used by Japanese field workers to decoratively mend patches in work clothes. Traditional Sashiko designs are based upon motifs found in nature and are left intentionally simple and unadorned. Because of its classic simplicity and form, Sashiko is an ideal machine technique for entry level sewers, but can also provide designs challenging enough for the advanced stitcher.

MACHINE SET-UP

- ♦ **Stitch:** Straight, L — 3½–4
- ♦ **Presser Foot:** Open or clear embroidery foot
- ♦ **Needles:** Topstitch needle, size #100
- ♦ **Threads:** Needle — Topstitching threads
    Bobbin — All-purpose polyester, color-matched
    to needle thread or fabric
- ♦ **Tension:** Normal to slightly tightened

FABRIC CHOICES:

Deep, indigo blue denim for a traditional Sashiko look. However, equally beautiful results can be obtained by using raw silks and medium weight woolens.

ADDITIONAL SUPPLIES:

- ♦ Fusible interfacing
- ♦ Tear–away stabilizer
- ♦ White fabric pencil
- ♦ Muslin bag with baby powder

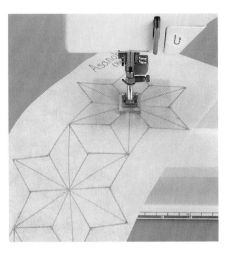

1 With careful planning and a chalk marker, divide your project into different sections to be embroidered. Because Sashiko is stitch intensive, design and stitch a double row of straight stitches between each section. These stitched divisions provide an "eye break", allowing your eye to travel from section to section, resting on straight stitches in between.

2 There are many wonderful Sashiko design books available. Trace the desired design on a piece of crisp, tear-away stabilizer. Using an unthreaded needle, sew through the design, leaving small perforations on the marked lines.

3 Position the design on the right side of the fabric. Using a small, powder–filled muslin bag, pounce the powder through the holes transferring the design to the fabric.

continued

4 Connect the powder dots with a marking pencil before sewing.

5 Test sew a sample design on an interfaced fabric scrap. Adjust the stitch length and tension, if necessary. Straight-stitch around the design, trying to complete the pattern with as long a line of continuous stitches as possible.

6 Leave long thread tails at the beginning and end of each row of stitches. Draw the tails to the wrong side, knot, and secure with seam sealant. Clip the threads when dry.

Tips Experiment with Sashiko stitching using decorative stitches. Remember, topstitching thread is much thicker than regular sewing thread. Select open stitch patterns to avoid thread jamming. A layer of tear-away stabilizer may also be needed with some of the stitch patterns to avoid puckers. Remove all the stabilizer when the stitching is completed.

QUILTING STYLES, TRAPUNTO

A unique quilting style and a variation of traditional outline quilting, trapunto involves just stuffing certain areas for a three-dimensional raised effect. Use either a preprinted fabric or create a design of your own to fill. A traditional hand quilting technique, trapunto can easily be achieved on your sewing machine.

MACHINE SET-UP

♦ **Stitch:** Straight
♦ **Presser Foot:** Darning or free-motion foot
♦ **Needles:** Match to fabric
♦ **Threads:** Needle — Monofilament
   Bobbin — 60 wt. cotton embroidery
♦ **Tension:** Slightly loosened needle
♦ **Feed Dogs:** Down
♦ **Optional:** Engage needle down function

FABRIC CHOICES:

Preprinted decorator fabric, larger designs best
Firm solid-colored fabrics

ADDITIONAL SUPPLIES:

♦ Puffy batting
♦ Thermal fleece
♦ Sharp scissors
♦ Quilt pins

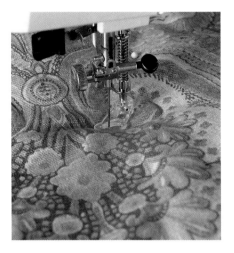

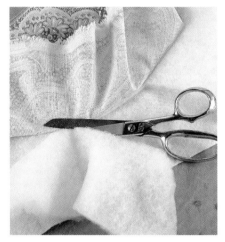

1 Place the puffy batting behind the area on the preprinted fabric for the trapunto. Add thermal fleece to the back. Pin at intervals using the longer quilt pins.

2 Remembering to lower the feed dogs, thread the machine with monofilament thread and attach the darning foot. Take a few stitches in place to lock the monofilament thread. Begin outlining the design for the trapunto. (Note: The closer together the lines of stitching in the design, the less "puffy" and obvious the trapunto will be.)

3 After the outline stitching is completed, trim away the puffy batting from the areas not stitched.

continued

4 To increase the effect of the trapunto, follow the instructions for "Stippling, Basic," and stitch outside the puffy area.

Tip To use this technique on solid-colored fabrics, trace your design on a tear-away stabilizer. Layer the fabric and batting and stitch from the back. Remove the stabilizer and cut away the batting. Since you are sewing from the reverse, a cotton or rayon embroidery thread may be used in the bobbin for a different effect.

RUCHING

Ruching is a form of gathering through the middle of a strip of ribbon or fabric. This strip is then applied as a surface element on the garment or home decorating project. Often rows of ruching were used around the hems of ladies gowns during the Victorian era. Simple and easy to stitch, ruching adds an extra textural touch to your sewing project.

MACHINE SET-UP

♦ **Stitch:** Step One: Straight, L — 5
　　　　Step Two: Straight, L — 2½
♦ **Presser Foot:** Step One: Gathering foot
　　　　Step Two: Open or clear embroidery foot
♦ **Needles:** Match to fabric
♦ **Threads:** Needle and bobbin — All-purpose polyester
♦ **Tension:** Tighten the needle

FABRIC CHOICES:

Soft, lightweight fabrics gather more easily

ADDITIONAL SUPPLIES:

♦ Air- or water-soluble fabric marker

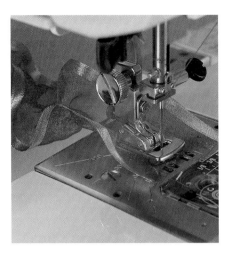

1 Adjust your machine according to the setting for Step One. Test the tightness of the gathering on a sample before starting your project. (Note: The longer the stitch length, the more gathers.)

2 Finish the raw edges of the fabric strip with a rolled or turned hem before gathering, if necessary.

3 Mark the center of your fabric strip or ribbon with the marking pen. Begin stitching following the marking.

4 Once the strip is gathered, pin it to the project turning in any raw ends. Select the setting and presser foot for Step Two and stitch the strip down.

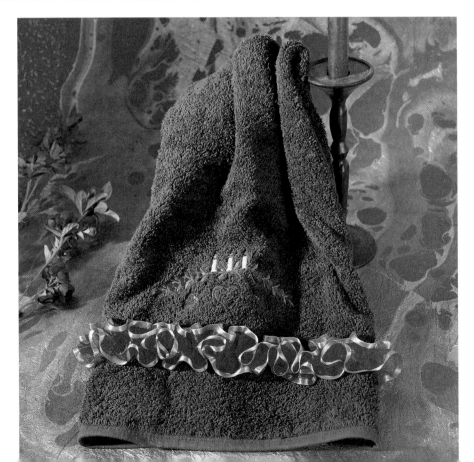

RUFFLING

The ruffler attachment is a very versatile piece of equipment for your sewing machine. Used with the straight stitch, gathers and pleats can be stitched in intervals or continuously based on the selected ruffler setting. When gathering long lengths of fabric, the ruffler attachment becomes invaluable to every sewer.

MACHINE SET-UP

- ♦ **Stitch:** Straight, L — the shorter the length, the fuller the gathers; the longer the stitch, the deeper the pleat
- ♦ **Presser Foot:** Ruffler attachment
- ♦ **Needles:** Universal needle, size #80
- ♦ **Threads:** Needle and bobbin — All-purpose polyester
- ♦ **Tension:** Normal to slightly loosened needle
- ♦ **Optional:** Adjust ruffler according to final result desired

FABRIC CHOICES:

Cottons or sheers

1 Review the components of your ruffler comparing the parts with the labeled photo shown here.

A. The separator blade—blue blade that guides the fabric above the feed dogs

B. The ruffler blade—upper blue blade pushes the fabric

C. The separator slots—used to hold and separate fabrics or trims

D. The adjusting gauge—screw in or out for range of depth of ruffle or pleat

E. The adjusting lever—adjusts to ruffle or pleat every 1, 6, or 12 stitches; can be disengaged for straight stitching

F. The fork arm—fits over needle clamp screw

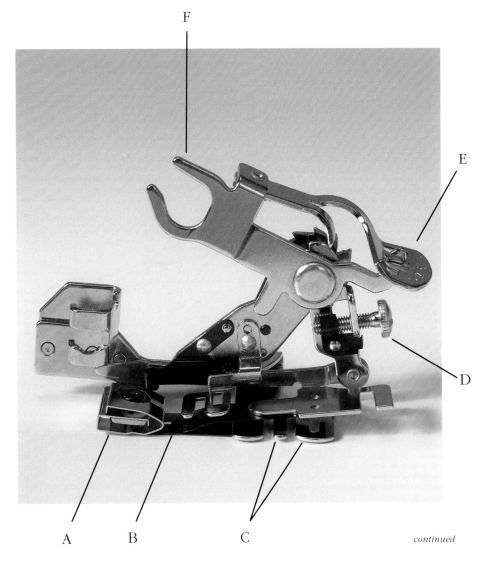

continued

2 For simple ruffling, fold a strip of fabric in half and press. Set the adjusting gauge for a long stitch and the adjusting lever to 1. Set your stitch length between 1 and 5.

3 Place the fabric between the blue blades and toward the back. Begin stitching. Shorten the stitch length as necessary.

4 To attach a ruffle to a flat piece of fabric, place the flat fabric below the blue blades. Insert the fabric to be ruffled in the same manner in Step 3.

5 To insert a ruffle between two pieces of fabric, set up the fabric pieces as in Step 4. Add the second flat piece of fabric above the top blade and in the separator slots. (Note: Hold the top fabric in your left hand and pull the bottom fabric slightly to the right to keep the layers aligned.)

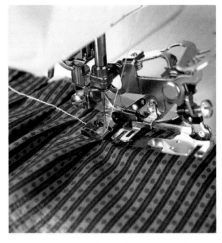

6 It is possible to ruffle or pleat 1 ½" in from the edge of your strip. Hem both edges of the strip in the manner desired. With right side up, slide the strip between the blades and to the right as far as possible. Stitch guiding evenly.

7 For pleating, set the adjusting gauge to a long stitch. Set the adjusting lever to every 6 or 12 stitches. The stitch length on your machine will regulate the distance between the pleats.

8 Place the fabric between the blue blades and begin stitching. To sew deeper pleats adjust the gauge to a longer setting.

Tip Estimate the yardage needed for ruffling before beginning your project by sewing a sample strip. Measure your beginning flat piece prior to ruffling; measure after ruffling to determine just how much fabric is needed.

For double-layer, sheer fabrics, fold the strip in half and clean-finish the raw edges with your serger or a zig zag stitch to control the fabric better under the ruffler.

SCALLOPS, OFF-THE-EDGE

Discover the simple ease of creating lace-like tatting trim with your sewing machine. Combine a basic satin stitch scallop, filler cord, embroidery threads, and tear-away stabilizer to sew delicate off-the-edge scallops. Sewn mainly on the stabilizer, the satin stitch scallop is strengthened by trapping a filler cord between the needle and bobbin threads. Sewn onto a finished edge, this trim adds a nice touch to any sewing project.

MACHINE SET-UP

- **Stitch:** Satin stitch scallop, size or width as desired
- **Presser Foot:** Embroidery foot or foot with a guide for fine cords
- **Needles:** Embroidery needle, size #75–#90
- **Threads:** Needle — Cotton or rayon embroidery threads
  Bobbin — Same as needle or all-purpose polyester
  Filler cord — Topstitching thread or gimp cord
- **Tension:** Normal

FABRIC CHOICES:

As desired

ADDITIONAL SUPPLIES:

- Crisp tear-away stabilizer
- Air- or water-soluble fabric marker
- Seam sealant

1 Back the edge to be scalloped with a strip of tear-away stabilizer, extending it at least 1" away from the fabric's finished edge. Thread the hole in the embroidery foot with the filler cord or feed the cord over the front bar of the foot leaving a 6" tail behind the foot.

2 Select your satin stitch scallop pattern. Slowly begin to sew the scallops. Position the fabric so that the tips of the scallop bite into the fabric and the curved edge of the scallop sews onto the stabilizer. The filler cord will be caught in the thread and guided by the presser foot.

3 After completing a single row, carefully remove the tear-away stabilizer from behind and below the stitched scallops. Hold onto the sewn scallop while removing the stabilizer for added support. Trim any excess stabilizer with your embroidery scissors.

4 Multiple rows of scallops can be added to the edge. Prepare the fabric and machine set-up as for single row scallops, adding a slightly wider piece of tear-away stabilizer underneath the folded fabric edge. (Note: Select an extra-crisp tear-away to firmly stabilize the scallops beyond the first row where they are sewn on stabilizer only.)

continued

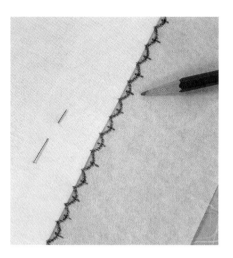

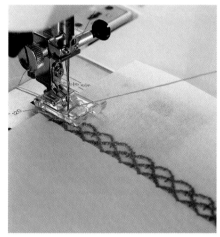

5 Stitch the first row of scallops. Using a fade-away marker, mark the center of each sewn scallop to help position the successive rows of scallops for an even pattern.

6 Sew any consecutive rows of scallops, beginning at the halfway point of the first scallop in the previous row.

7 Very carefully remove the stabilizer, holding onto the scallops for support while tearing. Trim away any excess "whiskers" from the stabilizer.

Tip Color-match the needle and bobbin threads and filler cord, as closely as possible, for the best results. "Color-in" any impossible-to-remove pieces of stabilizer with a matching permanent marker.

Coat sewn scallops *lightly* with seam sealant. Trim any "whiskers" from the edge when dry.

SCALLOPS, DOUBLE SATIN STITCH

The most refined scallops are sewn with a double edge. Even a beginner with very basic sewing machine knowledge can experience first-time success with this technique. Beautiful, whisker-free scalloped edges are a delightful and elegant finishing touch on any garment or home decorating project.

MACHINE SET-UP

- **Stitch:** Step One: Preprogrammed satin stitch scallop
  Step Two: Zig zag, L — $\frac{1}{2}$, W — $2\frac{1}{2}$–3
- **Presser Foot:** Open embroidery foot
- **Needles:** Universal needle, size #80
- **Threads:** Needle — Rayon embroidery
  Bobbin — All-purpose polyester, color matched to needle
- **Tension:** Slightly loosened needle
- **Optional:** Engage needle down function

FABRIC CHOICES:

Firm wovens, such as linen, batiste, or broadcloth

ADDITIONAL SUPPLIES:

- Air- or water-soluble fabric marker
- Clear ruler
- Seam sealant
- Spray starch
- Fine-tipped embroidery scissors
- Lightweight tear-away stabilizer

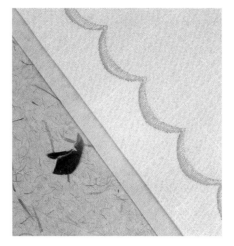

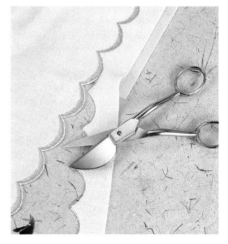

1 Spray-starch the area to be scalloped. Using a clear ruler and marker, draw a stitching guideline approximately ½"–1" from the edge of the fabric. Place a single or double layer of tear-away stabilizer under the stitching line.

2 Sew the first row of scallops.

3 Carefully remove the stabilizer. Coat the lower edge of the scallop stitch with seam sealant. Once the sealant is completely dry, trim closely to the lower edge.

continued

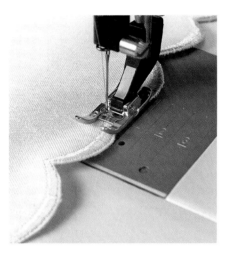

4 Reset the machine using the settings for Step Two. Zig zag along the trimmed edge following the curve. The left swing of the needle should fall into the fabric and the right just off the edge. This will encase the trimmed edge producing a clean-finished, professional result.

Tip Add a color accent to the edge by choosing a contrasting color of thread for the second row of stitches.

SILK RIBBON MACHINE EMBROIDERY, BOBBINWORK

Silk ribbon machine embroidery stitched from the wrong side adds a different dimension to your sewing handiwork. The silk ribbon is wound onto the bobbin and the design is sewn from the reverse.

MACHINE SET-UP

- ♦ **Stitch:** Simple, open-design stitches
- ♦ **Presser Foot:** Open or clear embroidery foot
- ♦ **Needles:** Universal needle, size #80
- ♦ **Threads:** Needle — Monofilament or all-purpose polyester, color matched to silk ribbon
  Bobbin — ONLY 2mm or 4mm silk ribbon, hand-wound on empty bobbin
- ♦ **Tension:** Normal to slightly tightened needle

FABRIC CHOICES:

Tightly woven, luxurious fabrics such as silk dupioni, moirés and jacquards are ideal. However, varied fabrics from chambray to knits can provide an equally interesting backdrop for these beautiful ribbons.

ADDITIONAL SUPPLIES:

- ♦ 2mm or 4mm silk ribbon
- ♦ Secondary bobbin case
- ♦ Spring-loaded or wooden embroidery hoop
- ♦ Fusible knit interfacing
- ♦ Air- or water-soluble fabric marker
- ♦ Large–eyed hand sewing needle

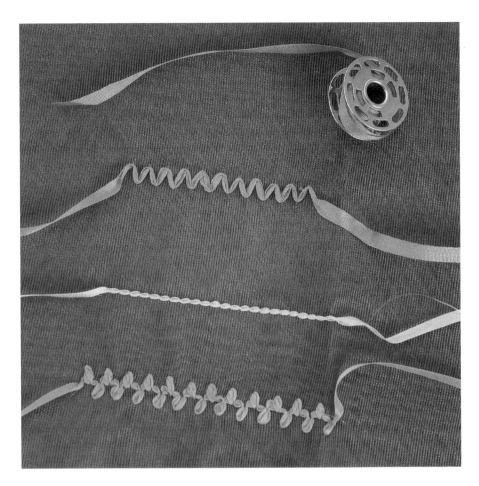

1 Select an open–designed, simple stitch, such as a straight, zig zag, or feather stitch. Follow Step 1 instructions for "Silk Ribbon Machine Embroidery, Couched". Place the fabric in the hoop wrong side up.

2 Mark the placement on the wrong side of the fabric. Stitch at a slow, even speed. Pull the ribbon tails to the wrong side and weave as in Step 5.

SILK RIBBON MACHINE EMBROIDERY, COUCHED

Beautiful silk ribbon bouquets can easily be stitched with deceptively simple machine techniques. Adapting this traditional Victorian handwork mainstay to modern sewing machine stitches is achieved by using two different techniques. Silk ribbons can either be couched from the right side of the fabric using free-motion sewing, or wound onto a bobbin and sewn from the wrong side of the fabric using preset stitch patterns. Both techniques guarantee to make a silk ribbon lover of every sewer.

MACHINE SET-UP

- ◆ **Stitch:** Straight
- ◆ **Presser Foot:** None
- ◆ **Needles:** Universal needle, size #80
- ◆ **Threads:** Needle — Monofilament
  Bobbin — All-purpose polyester, color matched to fabric
- ◆ **Tension:** Normal

FABRIC CHOICES:

Tightly woven, luxurious fabrics such as silk dupioni, moirés and jacquards are ideal. However, varied fabrics from chambray to knits can provide an equally interesting backdrop for these beautiful ribbons.

ADDITIONAL SUPPLIES:

- ◆ Silk ribbons in any size available
- ◆ Spring-loaded or wooden embroidery hoop
- ◆ Stiletto
- ◆ Fusible knit interfacing
- ◆ Air- or water-soluble fabric marker
- ◆ Large–eyed hand sewing needle

 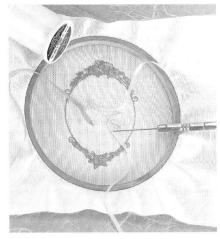

1 Press the fusible knit interfacing to the wrong side of the fabric to be embroidered. (Note: This interfacing layer helps support the ribbon stitches and eliminates puckering.)

2 Place the fused fabric, right side up, snugly into the hoop. Using a fade–away fabric marker, draw simple guidelines representing leaves and petals.

3 With a stiletto holding the ribbon close to the needle, secure one ribbon end with two stitches for the leaf base. With the ribbon moved to the side, sew to the leaf top. Bring the ribbon to the needle and tack in place with one or two stitches. Move the ribbon to the side again and sew back to the starting point at the leaf base. Bring the ribbon down and tack in place. Pivot and sew a second leaf if desired.

continued

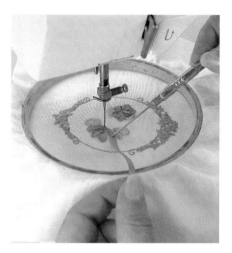

4 Sew a series of tacked loops clockwise in a circle to form a simple flower. Repeat as desired.

5 To finish, leave a 4" tail of ribbon after the last stitch. Thread the ribbon tail through a large-eye needle and pull to the wrong side. Weave the tail through the bobbin stitches and the interfacing layer. Clip the tail.

SHIRRING, BASIC

Horizontal, parallel rows of tightly shirred gathers are used as decorative inserts in yokes, cuffs, and bodices. Traditionally, one layer of a soft fabric is gathered or shirred on a pleating machine. Similar results can be achieved with a twin needle, filler cord, and a special presser foot. There are many ways to duplicate the look of traditional hand-smocking created with a pleater machine by using a home sewing machine. On the following pages, four techniques, all simple and all different, are listed. Have fun experimenting!

MACHINE SET-UP

- **Stitch:** Straight, L — 2½
- **Presser Foot:** 5 groove pintuck foot
- **Needles:** Double needle, size #1.6/70 or #2.0/80
- **Threads:** Needles and bobbin — All-purpose polyester Filler — Gimp or topstitching thread
- **Tension:** Normal

FABRIC CHOICES:

Soft fabrics, such as fine batiste, cotton lawn, lightweight silks, and rayons

ADDITIONAL SUPPLIES:

- Air- or water-soluble fabric or chalk marker
- Clear ruler
- Dental floss threader
- Quilting guide bar
- Fusible knit interfacing

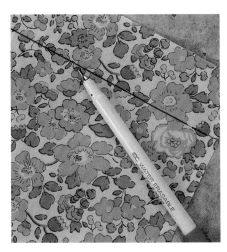

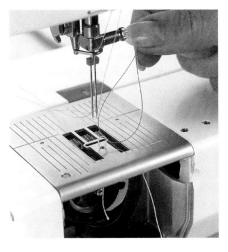

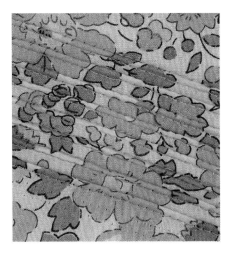

1 Cut the fabric 2½–3 times the desired finished shirred width. Using a fade-away fabric or a chalk marker, draw in the first stitching line. Set up your machine with the twin needles and pintuck foot with a quilting guide, if desired.

2 Using a dental floss threader, guide the filler cord through the opened bobbin case door and up through the small round opening found in the throat plate or check your sewing machine manual for the pintuck set-up for your machine. Pull about 6" of filler cord to the back of the machine.

3 Stitch a row of filled tucks on top of the drawn line, leaving a 6" tail on each edge of the fabric. Using the grooves on the underside of the pintuck foot, or spacing provided by the quilting bar, sew as many successive rows of filled tucks as desired. Clip the needle and bobbin thread tails on each side, leaving the filler cords.

continued

 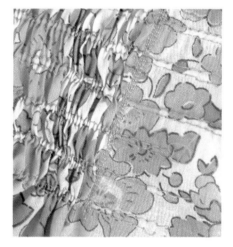 

4 Knot the rows of filler cord along one side. Pull the loose filler cord tails, creating a shirred panel of fabric. Adjust the gathers evenly and knot the tails.

5 Flatten the fabric in the seam allowance. Using a very short stitch length, zig zag across the pulled filler cords, securing them to the fabric. Steam the fabric to set the gathers.

6 If desired, further secure the gathered fabric by fusing a piece of weft insertion or fusible tricot interfacing to the wrong side of the smocking.

SHIRRING, ELASTIC

Shirring with built-in stretch can be sewn many ways. Two of the easiest methods are described here. Both gathering techniques are perfect for children's wear and cuff and neckline areas, eliminating the need for garment fasteners.

Method 1 uses twin needles to zig zag over narrow elastic cord that is machine-fed through a hole in the throat plate. The second method uses fine elastic cord as the bobbin thread to stitch gathers.

MACHINE SET-UP

Twin Needle Elastic Shirring
- **Stitch:** Zig zag, L — 4, W — 2½
- **Presser Foot:** Gathering foot, quilting guide, all-purpose foot
- **Needles:** Double needle, size #2.0/80
- **Threads:** Needle and bobbin — All-purpose polyester
  Filler — Fine, spooled elastic
- **Tension:** Normal to slightly tightened needle
- **Optional:** Engage double needle limitation

Elastic Bobbin Shirring
- **Stitch:** Straight, L — 3
- **Presser Foot:** All-purpose foot, quilting guide
- **Needles:** Match to fabric
- **Threads**: Needle — All-purpose polyester
  Bobbin — Fine, spooled elastic with good recovery
- **Tension:** Normal

FABRIC CHOICES:

Soft, lightweight fabrics

ADDITIONAL SUPPLIES:

- Dental floss threader
- Air- or water-soluble fabric or chalk marker

Method 1 — Twin Needle Elastic Shirring

1 Cut the fabric 2½–3 times the desired finished shirred piece needed. Insert the twin needles, quilting guide, and gathering foot onto the sewing machine.

Using a dental floss threader, guide the elastic cord through the opened bobbin case door and up through the small round opening in the throat plate, or use the pin-tuck plate for your machine. Leave a 6" tail behind the presser foot. Draw a guideline for the first row of stitching.

2 Zig zag over the drawn line, catching the elastic cord with the bobbin threads as you sew. Leave a 3" tail of threads and elastic at the end of each row.

3 Adjust the quilting guide bar or use the outer edge of the gathering foot to measure for additional rows of sewing. Stitch as many rows as you desire.

continued

239

4 From the right side, steam the shirred rows. The heat of the steam will cause the elastic to draw up, creating more shirring. (Note: If additional fullness is desired, the elastic cords can be pulled by hand to increase the gathering effect.)

5 Straight-stitch at the left- and right-hand sides to secure the cords and gathers.

Method 2 — Elastic Bobbin Shirring

1 Hand-wind the elastic cord onto an empty bobbin. Wrap evenly, stretching the elastic cord slightly while winding. Insert the bobbin into a secondary bobbin case, or by-pass the tension in the bobbin area. Loosen the tension set screw on the bobbin case so that the elastic cord unwinds freely. Cut the fabric to be gathered 3–4 times the desired finished width. Be generous. Draw the first guideline for shirring.

2 With right side up, position the presser foot on the drawn line. Stitch the first row of shirring. The fabric will automatically shirr due to the tightened tension on the elastic in the bobbin.

3 Adjust the quilting guide for successive rows. Sew multiple rows of elastic shirring. Steam the fabric to increase the fullness. Allow the fabric to rest overnight to complete drawing in. Stitch at each end of the shirring to secure the gathers.

SMOCKING, DECORATIVE ONE-STEP

Decoratively sew and gather fabrics in one step by using a gathering foot, a decorative stitch, and tightened needle tension. Utility stitches, such as the jersey stretch and honeycomb stitches, take on new creative beauty when sewn in rayon threads upon gently smocked yardage. This two-in-one-step stable smocking technique is a timesaver for quick shirred accents on your next sewing project.

MACHINE SET-UP

- **Stitch:** Stretch jersey or honeycomb stitch, L — slightly longer, W — Preset
- **Presser Foot:** Gathering foot, quilting guide
- **Needles:** Universal needle, size #80 or match to fabric
- **Threads:** Needle — All-purpose polyester, rayon or cotton embroidery
  Bobbin — All-purpose polyester
- **Tension:** Slightly to moderately tightened needle
- **Optional:** Decrease motor speed

FABRIC CHOICES:

Lightweight, drapable fabrics, such as batiste, fine cottons, silks, and rayon

ADDITIONAL SUPPLIES:

- Air- or water-soluble fabric or chalk marker
- Clear ruler
- Fusible knit interfacing

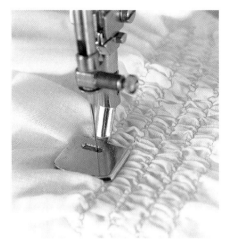

1 Cut the fabric at least two times the desired finished width. Increase the needle tension at least two numbers above normal. Draw a horizontal guideline to aid in sewing the first row. (Note: Smocking is sewn on a single layer of fabric. Due to the variation in fabric weights and machine tensions, it's recommended to sew a test sample of a few rows of smocking to fine-tune the amount of shirring produced at a given stitch length and tension.)

2 Stitch along the drawn line, gathering the fabric while sewing a decorative stitch. The bottom on the gathering foot working with the increased needle tension will create tiny, delicate gathers.

3 Adjust the quilting guide or use the edge of the presser foot to position when sewing additional rows. Sew as many rows as desired. (Note: The closer together the rows, the more gathering will appear.)

4 Steam the sewn rows when completed. If desired, secure the shirring by fusing tricot or weft insertion interfacing to the wrong side of the smocking.

SMOCKING, ON PRE-PLEATED YARDAGE

Handwork smocking stitches on fine batiste, which has been gathered into tiny pleats, has long been a mainstay of heirloom sewing. Flat fabric is pleated into bands using a multi-needle pleating machine. The pleats are then over-embroidered using embroidery floss and traditional hand stitches. Today's sewing machines can provide the machine embroiderer limitless options using the same pre-pleated yardage.

MACHINE SET-UP

- **Stitch:** Preprogrammed cross stitches, small satin stitch bars, hearts, scrolls, flowers, or any decorative pattern with a hand-embroidered appearance
- **Presser Foot:** Open embroidery foot
- **Needles:** Universal needle, size #90 or machine embroidery needle, size #90
- **Threads:** Needle — 30 or 40 wt. cotton or rayon embroidery
  Bobbin — 60 wt. cotton embroidery
- **Tension:** Normal
- **Optional:** Engage needle down function

FABRIC CHOICES:

Fine, lightweight natural fibers, such as 100% cotton batiste, pre-pleated on a multi-needle pleating machine

ADDITIONAL SUPPLIES:

- Fusible, lightweight woven interfacing
- Optional: Water-soluble stabilizer

1 Adjust the fabric on the pre-pleated yardage to yield a piece slightly larger than needed for the project. Cut and fuse a piece of lightweight, woven interfacing to the wrong side of the pleated band. This interfacing will support and stabilize the pleats, preventing them from opening during embroidery or completely releasing while wearing the garment.

2 Pre-plan your overall design on a piece of paper to create a pleasing embroidered band. Refer to domestic and international heirloom sewing magazines or pleating plates for inspiration and design ideas.

3 From the right side, layer the water-soluble stabilizer over the fabric band or begin to sew directly on top of the pleats. The fused interfacing will help keep the pleating straight and secure. Stitch your design either beginning from the top working to the bottom, or from the middle working out from the center to create a balanced design. Sew at a reduced, medium speed. Use the point of a seam ripper, if it's necessary to adjust any wayward pleats while sewing.

continued

4 Remove any stabilizer from the top and lightly steam the finished embroidered band. Remove any unnecessary pleating threads to allow the embroidered band to appear as close to the released gathers as possible.

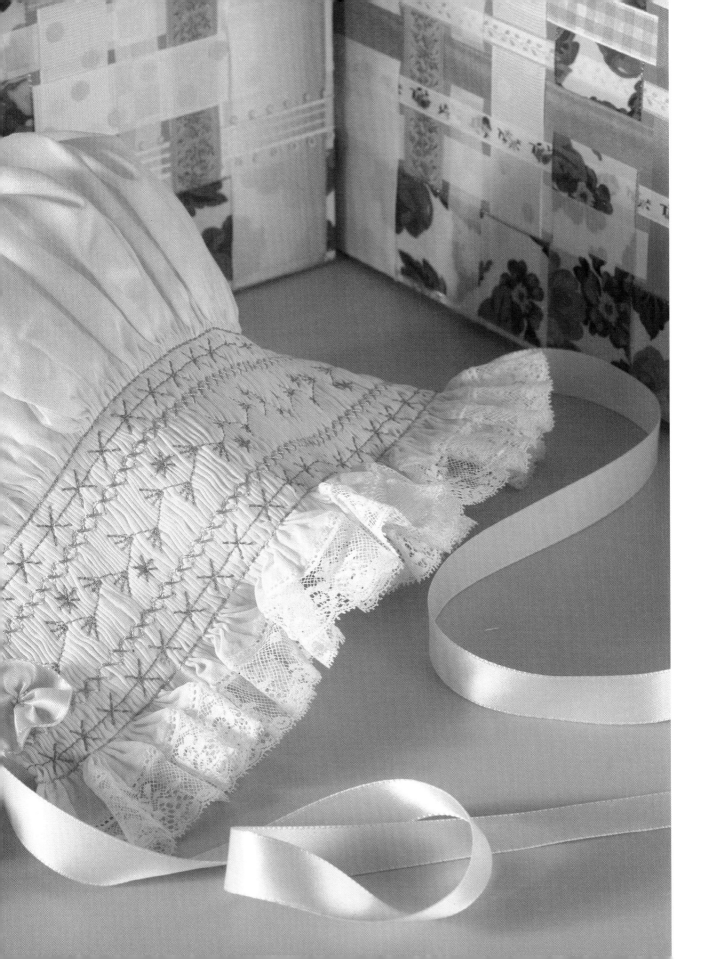

SMYRNA EMBROIDERY

Smyrna, or wool embroidery, is the perfect textural technique to use on upholstery-weight fabrics. A chenille-like surface texture is created using yarns and monofilament thread. The stitched loops are clipped, then fluffed up for this interesting three-dimensional effect. It's a wonderful technique for pillows, lap robes, or garments, using the designs woven into the fabrics as your base.

MACHINE SET-UP

♦ **Stitch:** Straight
♦ **Presser Foot:** Free-motion, darning, or open darning foot
♦ **Needles:** Universal needle, size #80
♦ **Threads:** Needle — Monofilament
    Bobbin — All-purpose polyester
♦ **Tension:** Normal to slightly loosened needle
♦ **Feed Dogs:** Lowered
♦ **Optional:** Engage needle down function

FABRIC CHOICES:

Stable jacquard upholstery or home decorating fabric

ADDITIONAL SUPPLIES:

♦ Wool or acrylic yarn
♦ Spring-loaded or wooden embroidery hoop
♦ Very small crochet hook
♦ Long tweezers
♦ Embroidery scissors
♦ Optional: Tear-away stabilizer

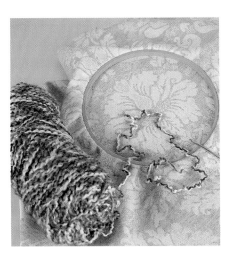

1 Select a section of the fabric and center the design in the hoop.

2 Beginning in one corner of the design, tack down the end of the yarn holding it with the tweezers. Stitch back and forth over the end; clip the threads close.

3 While holding the yarn in your left hand, with your right hand loop the yarn over the crochet hook and pull under the foot and in front of the needle. Take a few stitches to tack the yarn loop in place on the fabric.

continued

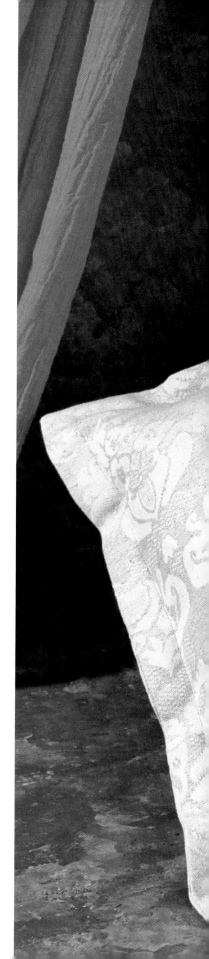

4 Fill in your design using the above technique. Keep the loops short and of equal height.

Tip Add dimensional detailing to the design by trimming the yarn at different heights. Or mix different types of yarns for interest.

5 Clip the loops and fluff up the yarn for a chenille-like effect. For added textural interest, leave some loops unclipped.

STIPPLING, BASIC

Stippling is a free-motion background-quilting technique that is easy to do and fun to learn. Use this texturizing technique on garments as well as home decorating items. The closer together the stitching, the flatter the batting or filler becomes. Stippling is also a fun way to become used to the free-motion aspect of your sewing machine as you really can't make any mistakes when sewing!

MACHINE SET-UP

- **Stitch:** Straight
- **Presser Foot:** Darning or free-motion foot
- **Needles:** Universal needle, size #80
- **Threads:** Needle — All-purpose polyester or monofilament
  Bobbin — All-purpose polyester
- **Tension:** Slightly loosened needle
- **Feed Dogs:** Lowered
- **Optional:** Adjust presser foot pressure for free-motion work

FABRIC CHOICES:

As desired

ADDITIONAL SUPPLIES:

- Fleece or quilt batting
- Quilt pins

1 Sandwich the fleece or batting between your layers of fabric. (Note: This technique is usually done just before the quilt is completed.) Pin at intervals to avoid the shifting of the layers.

2 If you are using monofilament thread, adjust the tension so the lower thread doesn't show. Begin stitching in a wavy-like motion moving the fabric back and forth. Swirl the stitching just like you were doodling on paper, keeping the swirls close together.

3 The final result should look like fine swirls all across the fabric. Do not overlap any lines of your stitching.

STIPPLING, ELASTIC

With elastic thread on the bobbin, use the stippling technique to create uniquely textured fabric. Full of stretch, this new fabric can be used for bodices, cuffs, waistline treatments, or insets in many garment designs. The fabric pulls up while you are sewing, giving it the three-dimensional effect.

MACHINE SET-UP

- ♦ **Stitch:** Straight
- ♦ **Presser Foot:** Darning or free-motion foot
- ♦ **Needles:** Match to fabric
- ♦ **Threads:** Needle — All-purpose polyester or monofilament
  Bobbin — Fine, spooled elastic
- ♦ **Tension:** Adjust as necessary
- ♦ **Feed Dogs:** Lowered
- ♦ **Optional:** Adjust presser foot pressure for free-motion work

FABRIC CHOICES:

Soft, pliable fabrics, such as lightweight cottons, single knits, gauze, washed denim, or crepe

ADDITIONAL SUPPLIES:

- ♦ Optional: Fusible knitt interfacing

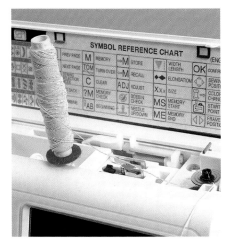

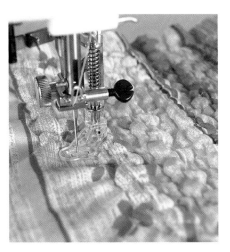

1 Carefully wind the elastic thread on your bobbin. By-pass the bobbin tension and wind directly from the spool to the bobbin guiding the thread with your finger.

2 Follow the instructions in Steps 2 and 3 for "Stippling, Basic". (Note: You may want to stabilize the fabric with a fusible tricot prior to sewing.)

3 The fabric will gather up while you are stitching.

***

Tip If using the elastic stippling technique on a garment, stipple the fabric first before you cut out the pattern pieces as the elastic thread will gather the fabric up quite a bit.

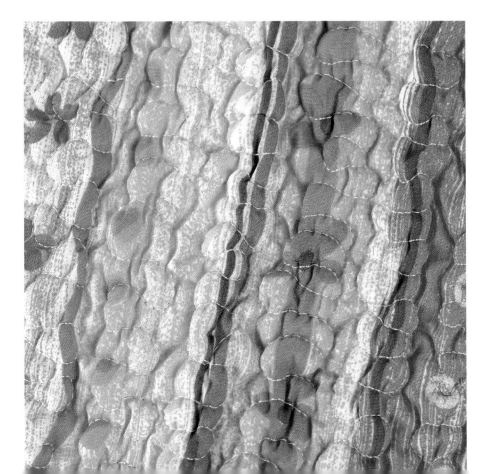

THREAD PAINTING

Thread painting is a form of free-motion embroidery with the designs filled in completely with thread. You are literally painting with your sewing machine, needle, and thread. Wonderful designs can be created just with a straight or zig zag stitch. Many sewing machines have built-in embroidery capabilities but this free-motion technique allows you the ability to create your very own designs.

MACHINE SET-UP

- **Stitch:** Straight, L — 2–2½ or zig zag, L — N/A, W — 2–5
- **Presser Foot:** Darning or free-motion foot
- **Needles:** Embroidery needle, size #80
- **Threads:** Needle — 30 wt., 40 wt., or 50 wt. cotton or rayon embroidery, metallic
  Bobbin — 60 wt. cottonembroidery
- **Tension:** Loosen needle
- **Feed Dogs:** Lowered
- **Optional:** Engage needle down function or adjust presser foot pressure for free-motion work

FABRIC CHOICES:

As desired

ADDITIONAL SUPPLIES:

- Tear-away stabilizer
- Spring-loaded or wooden embroidery hoop
- Air- or water-soluble fabric marker

1 Transfer the design to the fabric with your marking pen. Layer the fabric over the tear-away stabilizer and insert into the hoop. Make sure the fabric is taut.

2 Select the zig zag width appropriate to the size of the entire embroidery design. The wider the stitch the easier it is to use as a fill-in stitch.

3 Pull the bobbin thread up to the top and take a few stitches to lock the threads. Clip the thread tails close to the fabric. Begin stitching at a moderately fast speed, moving the hoop in an even, smooth motion, back and forth across the design. Fill in the design with your stitches trying not to form "rows" across the fabric. A more random uneven pattern is desired.

4 Change thread color and remember to lock stitches for detail work. Add any straight-stitching details or a narrow satin stitch outline to complete your design. Remove the tear-away stabilizer from the back and press.

continued

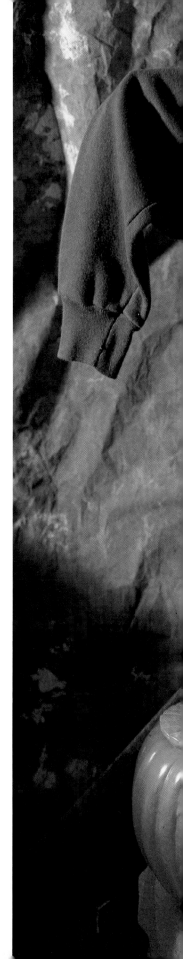

Tips As with all free-motion work, it is important to develop a steady rhythm when moving your hoop. Begin stitching on scrap fabric prior to starting your project to get "warmed up."

Sketch your design first and fill in the stitches in the direction desired. With thread painting, you have more freedom to rotate your hoop and change the direction of your stitches than with other free-motion techniques. A change of direction can provide shading and dimensional aspects to the design.

5 As with "Embroidery, Free-motion", a circular stitching technique can also be used for thread painting. Move the hoop in small circles overlapping the stitches. Fill in the entire design and then outline with a narrow satin stitch to define the shape.

TUCKS, MEXICAN

Add a little flair to your multiple rows of tucks by creating a wave-like treatment with a straight stitch. A more three-dimensional textural effect is achieved using this technique.

MACHINE SET-UP

- ♦ **Stitch:** Straight, L — 2–2½
- ♦ **Presser Foot:** All-purpose foot with quilting guide
- ♦ **Needles:** Match to fabric
- ♦ **Threads:** Needle and bobbin — All-purpose polyester
- ♦ **Tension:** Normal

FABRIC CHOICES:

As desired, though crisper fabrics work best

1 Begin by following all the steps in "Tucks, Single Needle" to create multiple, even rows of tucks across the fabric.

2 Beginning at one end, press all the tucks in one direction and stitch them down with a straight stitch.

3 Attach the quilting guide the desired distance from the needle. Pin the tucks in the opposite direction. Stitch the tucks down using the quilting guide to keep the stitching line even.

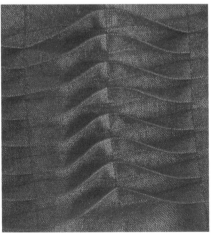

4 Repeat pinning and stitching the tucks in a back-and-forth direction across the width of the fabric, creating a wave effect.

TUCKS, PICOT-EDGED

A more delicate treatment for tucks is the picot-edged tuck. A simple, all-forward stretch or jersey stitch creates a fine, delicate edge finish on softer fabrics such as batiste or single knits. Add this fine detailing to a collar edge, slip edge, or knit top.

MACHINE SET-UP

♦ **Stitch:** Overlock, blindhem, or all-forward stretch stitch
♦ **Presser Foot:** All-purpose foot
♦ **Needles:** Match to fabric
♦ **Threads:** Needle and bobbin — 40 or 50 wt. cotton or rayon embroidery
♦ **Tension:** Normal to slightly loosened needle
♦ **Optional:** Mirror image if necessary for blindhem stitch

FABRIC CHOICES:

Fine, lightweight woven fabrics, such as batiste, single knits, or ribbing

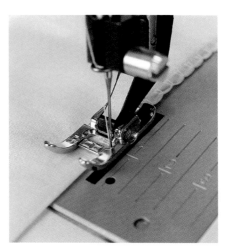

1 Follow Step 1 in "Tucks, Single Needle" if you are using woven fabrics to achieve straight tucks. For single knits or ribbing, fold and press the fabric for the tuck.

2 Select the appropriate stitch on your machine. (Note: Select a stitch with a right-swing zig zag and two or three straight stitches in between.) Place the fold of the tuck under the foot so the right-needle swing will fall off the fabric. Begin stitching. The configuration of the stitch will cause the fabric to pull in slightly at each zig zag, creating a scalloped-like effect on the edge.

Tip The picot-edged treatment is easy to duplicate on knit ribbing. Just like ready-to-wear, this picot edge adds a professional finish to your knit garment.

TUCKS, SINGLE NEEDLE

Simple folds of fabric stitched down with a straight stitch can add a quick decorative touch to any garment or home-decorating project. Tucks used at the hemline are perfect for the growing child — decorative yet functional. Release tucks can add more room in a garment, making it more comfortable to wear. Any width of tucks can be sewn for a variety of looks.

MACHINE SET-UP

♦ **Stitch:** Straight, L — 2–2½
♦ **Presser Foot:** All-purpose foot with quilting guide, ¼" foot
♦ **Needles:** Match to fabric
♦ **Threads:** Needle and bobbin — All-purpose polyester
♦ **Tension:** Normal

FABRIC CHOICES:

As desired

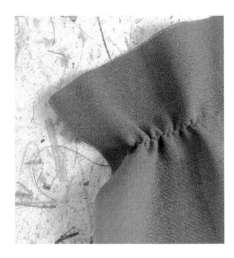

1 To achieve straight even tucks, pull a crosswise thread to find the straight of grain. Fold on the pulled thread line and press.

2 Sew narrow ¼" tucks by using the ¼" foot as your guide. Once the first tuck is sewn fold back the next tuck at the distance desired from the first.

3 Use the markings on your needle plate as another easy guide to measure the depth of your tucks. The edge of the fabric rides along the line on the needle plate. Move the needle position right or left for more variations.

4 For wide tucks, attach the quilt guide to the machine or presser foot. Measure the distance out from the needle to the guide for your tuck depth.

Tip To prevent your tucks from rippling when sewn, it is important to make sure you are sewing on the straight-of-grain. Pulling a thread is a quick simple way to achieve this result.

INDISPENSABLE TECHNIQUES

There are many sewing techniques that are

almost essential to all of your projects. Stitching

hem, seam, or edge finishes, buttonholes, or

zipper insertions becomes second nature once

you learn the procedure. Try them all, or

you may even need to add your own favorite

technique to the list if it is overlooked here!

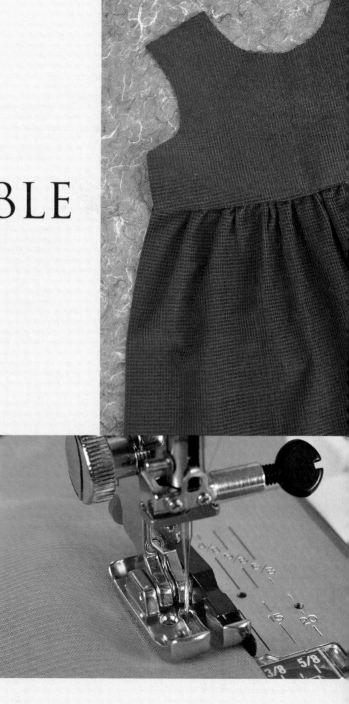

BIAS BINDING

Elegant and versatile, bias binding is an invaluable technique in any sewers' repertoire. Classic in its simplicity, bias binding can replace bulky neck and armhole facings in lightweight and sheer fabrics, serve as a hem finish, add color definition to a garment edge, or is the finishing touch to your latest quilt project.

MACHINE SET-UP

♦ **Stitch:** Straight
♦ **Presser Foot:** All-purpose or ¼" foot, edgestitch, zipper foot, open or clear embroidery foot
♦ **Needles:** Match to fabric
♦ **Threads:** Needle and bobbin — All-purpose polyester
♦ **Tension:** Normal
♦ **Optional:** Adjust needle position

FABRIC CHOICES:

Woven and knit fabrics

ADDITIONAL SUPPLIES:

♦ Bias tape makers in various sizes

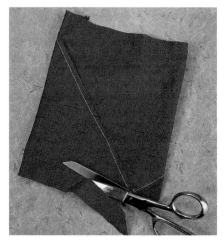

1 Fold a square of fabric in half diagonally, pressing in a crease. Cut the square into two triangles on the creased, diagonal line.

2 With right sides together, pin and sew the two triangles together using a ¼" seam allowance. Press the seam open. Your seamed fabric will look like a long parallelogram.

3 On the wrong side, mark the desired width of the bias strips. Trim away any unequal-width strip past the last full-width strip marked. With right sides together, match and sew the top and bottom short edges, offsetting by one strip width. You will be sewing a bias tube. Cut the bias strips from the tube, beginning at one end.

continued

4 Following the manufacturer's directions, insert the cut strips into the bias tape maker, pressing in the folded edges with an iron.

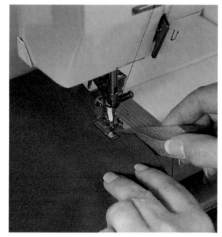

5 Open up the pressed bias tape. With right sides together, pin the bias tape to the fabric edge keeping the raw edges even. Using the creased fold as a guide, stitch the bias tape to the fabric edge.

6 Refold the tape along the crease lines and wrap the sewn strip around the edge. Press and pin in place. From the right side, stitch in the ditch, using an edgestitch or open embroidery foot, securing the loose edge of the tape underneath.

Tip If using the standard foot for stitching the bias, move the needle position to the right to yield a ¼" seam allowance.

When binding curved edges, pre-shape the bias binding using a steam iron to duplicate the curve of the edge being bound. Press carefully to avoid any stretching.

BUTTONHOLES, BOUND

Nothing says couture sewing as strongly as garments finished with bound buttonholes. Add subtle design accents though the use of contrast or striped fabrics for the buttonhole lips. Once the mainstay of fine tailoring classes, the simplified organza-patch method described here is foolproof and perfect for fabrics that fray easily.

FABRIC CHOICES:

Medium to heavyweight woven fabrics work best. Choose self-fabric or a contrasting fabric for the buttonhole lips. Interface the lips if the fabric weights differ.

MACHINE SET-UP

- **Stitch:** Straight, L — shorter than usual, approximately 2
- **Presser Foot:** All-purpose foot, open or clear embroidery foot or zipper foot
- **Needles:** Match to fabric
- **Threads:** Needle and bobbin — All-purpose polyester
- **Tension:** Normal
- **Optional:** Adjust needle position

ADDITIONAL SUPPLIES:

- Crisp, sheer organza
- Air- or water-soluble fabric chalk marker
- Fine, embroidery scissors
- Small amount of fusible web, slightly larger than organza patch
- Small amount of weft insertion fusible interfacing for back of buttonhole

1 Mark the right side of the garment for buttonhole placement. Cut a rectangle of weft insertion interfacing ½" longer and wider than the desired buttonhole. Fuse the interfacing piece to the wrong side at the buttonhole site.

Tip If using the standard presser foot, adjust the needle position to the right for a ¼" seam allowance.

2 Cut an organza rectangle approximately 1" larger than the buttonhole. Center the organza patch on the garment right side, at the marked buttonhole site. Mark the buttonhole length on the organza strip.

3 Sew in a rectangle ½" by the desired length of buttonhole, using small stitches. Slash through the center of the rectangle, stopping just short of the corners. Cut diagonally into the corners. Turn the organza patch to the wrong side through the slashed opening, creating a faced window. Press.

4 Cut two bias strips 1½" wide and 1" longer than the buttonhole window. With wrong sides together, fold the strips in half. Press.

5 Press two narrow strips of fusible web to the organza patch on the garment wrong side. Center and fuse the buttonhole

lips behind the window. Fold back the fashion fabric, exposing the triangular ends. Using a zipper foot, stitch the lips to the buttonhole sides.

6 Straight-stitch outside the buttonhole window, securing the lips to the window. Once the garment is completely lined, cut a slightly narrower buttonhole window in

the garment facing. Pin and whipstitch the two layers together.

BUTTONHOLES, CORDED

Eliminate gaping, frog's mouth buttonholes in knits or add extra strength to buttonholes sewn in heavy coating fabrics by adding cording. Most sewing machine manuals will have specific directions for this simple, yet very useful technique. The steps may be slightly different on each machine but worth the extra effort.

MACHINE SET-UP

♦ **Stitch:** Rectangle buttonhole style of your choice, L and W — Preset
♦ **Presser Foot:** Buttonhole foot recommended by manufacturer (Note: The foot must have a small finger on the front or back to hold the filler cord.)
♦ **Needles:** Match to fabric
♦ **Threads:** Needle and bobbin — All-purpose polyester
   Filler — Gimp or topstitching thread
♦ **Tension:** Slightly loosened needle
♦ **Optional:** Follow the manufacturer's instructions for your machine

FABRIC CHOICES:

As desired

ADDITIONAL SUPPLIES:

♦ Air- or water-soluble fabric or chalk marker
♦ Seam sealant
♦ Sharp embroidery scissors or buttonhole cutter & block

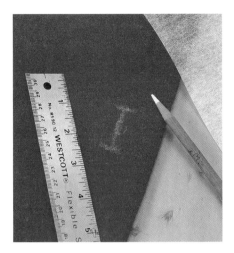

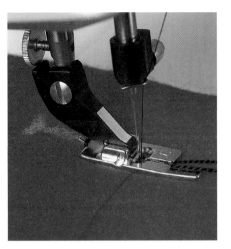

1 On the right side of the fabric, mark each buttonhole position. Cut a piece of filler cord two times the length of the desired buttonhole, plus 8".

2 Insert the needle into the fabric at the outer edge of the buttonhole. Raise the buttonhole foot and place the center of the filler cord over the small finger on the

buttonhole foot. Place the left and right sides of the cord in the tunnels under the foot.

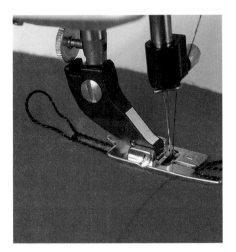

3 Sew the buttonhole. The cord will automatically feed underneath the foot and be encased in the zig zag of the buttonhole stitch. A

small loop of filler cord will remain at the front or back of the buttonhole, with the tails extending at the end.

4 Pull on the cord tails until the loop disappears. Feed the loose ends to the wrong side. Knot and dot the ends with seam sealant. Clip when dry.

BUTTONHOLES, DECORATIVE

Turn simple garment fasteners into tiny works of art with decorated buttonholes! Consider these slotted openings as "mini canvases" by adding decorative stitches, sewn either before or after the utilitarian buttonhole is created. Here's the place to experiment with thread colors and textures, too. Have fun!

MACHINE SET-UP

- **Stitch:** Any buttonhole style of choice
- **Presser Foot:** Buttonhole foot recommended for style of buttonhole chosen, open or clear embroidery foot
- **Needles:** Match to fabric
- **Threads:** Needle — All-purpose polyester, coordinating or contrasting cotton, rayon, variegated or metallic threads
  Bobbin — All-purpose polyester
- **Tension:** Slightly loosened needle
- **Optional:** Engage the single pattern and/or mirror imaging functions as needed for interesting design effects

FABRIC CHOICES:

Woven fabrics and stabilized knits

ADDITIONAL SUPPLIES:

- Air- or water-soluble fabric or chalk marker
- Seam sealant
- Fine embroidery scissors or buttonhole cutter & block
- Weft insertion interfacing
- Tear-away stabilizer

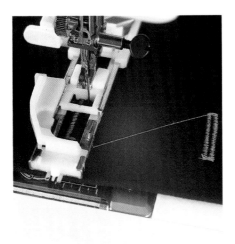

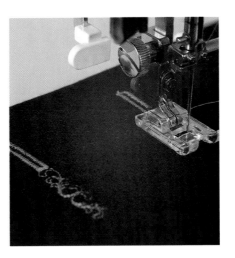

1 Mark each buttonhole position. Fuse a small rectangle of weft insertion interfacing to the wrong side of the garment at each buttonhole marking. Sew the desired buttonhole style.

2 Change to an open or clear embroidery foot. Select the desired decorative motif, using the single pattern or mirror image functions as needed. Sew the decorative pattern as close to the stitched buttonhole as possible, blending the two sets of sewing together. (Note: On some designs, it may be preferable to sew the decorative pattern first, then stitch the buttonhole over it.)

Tips When designing your decorative buttonholes, keep in mind that a button must also be included as part of the design.

Always sew a sample to fine-tune the size and shape of the decorative pattern chosen; how well it blends with the button to be used; and how a row of decorative buttonholes work into the overall garment design. You will also be able to determine if a layer of tear-away stabilizer is needed to support the decorative stitching.

BUTTONS, MACHINE-SEWN

Take the drudgery out of garment finishing by attaching drilled-hole buttons with a sewing machine. Buttons can be sewn on with a high or low thread shank for an incredibly strong connection. Most sewing machines have a button sew-on stitch pattern; however, a utility stitch, called the universal stitch, may also be used. Sew on charms, hooks and eyes, and jewels in much the same manner.

MACHINE SET-UP

- **Stitch:** Button sew-on or universal stitch, W — Preset or adjust the zig zag to accommodate the distance between the button's holes
- **Presser Foot:** Button sew-on foot
- **Needles:** Match to fabric
- **Threads:** Needle and bobbin — All-purpose polyester
- **Tension:** Normal
- **Optional:** Lower feed dogs

FABRIC CHOICES:

As desired

ADDITIONAL SUPPLIES:

- Drilled-hole buttons only
- Glue stick
- Air- or water-soluble fabric or chalk marker

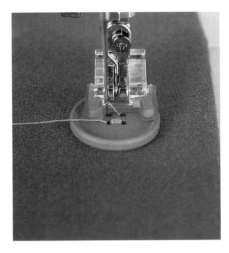

1 Using a chalk or fade-away fabric marker, indicate the button placement on the right side of the fabric. Rub a small amount of glue on the wrong side of the button, pressing it in place.

2 Select the button sew-on or universal stitch pattern. Place the button so the center of the foot is over the drilled holes. Check to make sure the zig zag width is correct. Complete the button sew-on pattern for 2- or 4-hole buttons.

3 Carefully remove the button and thread shank by raising the presser foot and pulling the work towards you. Pull all thread tails to the wrong side, knot, and clip.

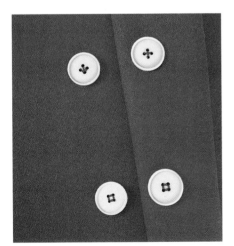

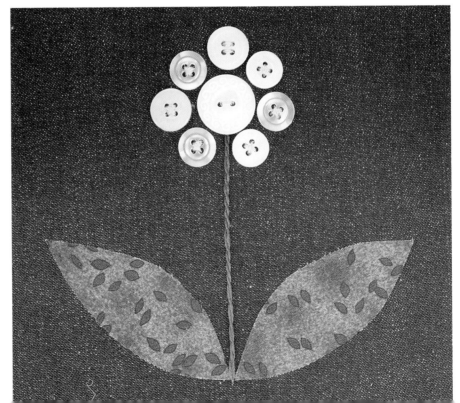

4 Experiment with different stitching designs or thread colors when attaching your buttons.

EDGE FINISHES, PICOT

Delicate, scallop shell-shaped, picot edges are as simple as reversing the sewing direction of your blindhem stitch. Use your mirror image function to flip the stitch and sew the straight portion onto the fabric with the zig zag portion sewing on and then off the finished fabric edge. The pull of the zig zag stitch back into the fabric will gently coax the fabric edge into little scallops. This is a popular edge finish on children's clothing, sportswear, and lingerie.

MACHINE SET-UP

- ◆ **Stitch:** Blindhem stitch, L and W — approximately 2½–3
- ◆ **Presser Foot:** Blindhem foot
- ◆ **Needles:** Match to fabric
- ◆ **Threads:** Needles and bobbin — All-purpose polyester
- ◆ **Tension:** Normal
- ◆ **Optional:** Engage mirror image function

FABRIC CHOICES:

Soft knits and woven fabrics are best

ADDITIONAL SUPPLIES:

- ◆ Spray starch

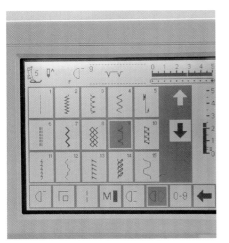

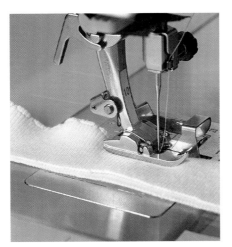

1 If needed, lightly spray-starch the area to be sewn. Select the blindhem stitch, assuring that the vertical (straight stitch) portion of the pattern sews onto the fabric and the needle swing of the zig zag sews off the finished edge. Engage the mirror image function if your sewing machine presets the stitch to sew in the opposite direction. (Note: Picot edges are sewn onto a clean-finished edge, such as seamed lingerie straps, T-shirt sleeves or bottom hems, and ribbed edges.

2 Place the finished edge of the fabric against the blade of the blindhem foot. Sew the straight stitches onto the fabric with the zig zag stitches sewing off. Adjust the width and length as desired.

281

EDGE FINISHES,
ROLLED

Finely stitched, rolled edges that rival serger hems can be simply sewn using a buttonhole foot. Stitched on a single layer of fabric using a zig zag stitch, the tunnel of thread and fabric travels in the groove on the bottom of the foot.

MACHINE SET-UP

- ♦ **Stitch:** Zig zag, L — ½, W — approximately 3
- ♦ **Presser Foot:** Buttonhole foot with grooves on the bottom
- ♦ **Needles:** Match to fabric
- ♦ **Threads:** Needle — All-purpose polyester, rayon, or cotton embroidery
  Bobbin — All-purpose polyester
- ♦ **Tension:** Slightly tightened needle
- ♦ **Optional:** Move needle to far-left needle position

FABRIC CHOICES:

Light- to medium weight woven fabrics

 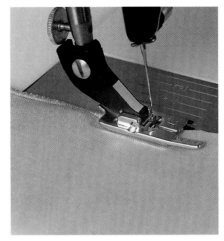

1 Position the raw edge of the fabric under the foot slightly to the right of center. Set the machine for a zig zag stitch and adjust the needle position.

2 Begin to sew the edge. The left swing of the needle will sew into the fabric; the right swing of the needle will sew just outside the cut edge.

3 As the needle swings back left, the thread will coax the fabric into a fine, rolled edge.

EDGE FINISHES, WIRE-EDGED

Customize your favorite fabrics into strips of unique wire-edged ribbon. Use a traditional buttonhole foot, 24–28 gauge wire, and a simple zig zag stitch to add structure to cut fabric bands.

MACHINE SET-UP

- **Stitch:** Zig zag, L — 1½, W — 3–5 depending upon fabric weight
- **Presser Foot:** Non-automatic buttonhole foot
- **Needles:** Universal needle, size #70 or #80
- **Threads:** Needle — All-purpose polyester, cotton or rayon embroidery
  Bobbin — All-purpose polyester or 60 wt. cotton embroidery, color matched to needle thread
- **Tension:** Normal
- **Optional:** Move needle position to half left

FABRIC CHOICES:

Light- to medium weight wovens, such as decorator fabrics, laces, sheers or cottons. Striped cotton prints are ideal for perfect preprinted ribbon strips.

ADDITIONAL SUPPLIES:

- 24–28 gauge wire
- Craft scissors or wire cutters
- Seam sealant
- Optional: Spray starch

1 Cut the fabric into the desired width for ribbon strips. Spray-starch lightweight fabrics to add extra body and to feed evenly.

2 Place the fabric strip, wrong side up, underneath the presser foot. The cut edge should be centered in the opening on the foot. Thread the wire underneath the foot, slightly to the left of the cut edge. Begin to zig zag over the wire. The left swing of the zig zag stitch should fall into the fabric, the right swing off the fabric. When the needle swings to the left, the edge of the fabric will curl over the wire, creating a thread and fabric tunnel. Zig zag down both long edges of the fabric. Apply seam sealant at all ends to secure.

Tip When stitching wire edges on laces or sheers, sew each side two times. The first pass of stitching secures the wire and the second traps the fabric whiskers in the rolled hem for a smooth, professional finish.

GATHERING, BASIC TECHNIQUE

Gathering fabric adds fullness to a garment, giving it a soft, feminine look. Gathered skirts, puffed sleeves, and ruffles are all design elements that require additional fabric with small, even gathers or tucks to make it the needed size. A long stitch length is used so the bobbin thread can be easily pulled to gather the fabric. Stitch several parallel rows of gathers to create a shirred look for yokes, bodices, and cuffs.

MACHINE SET-UP

- **Stitch:** Straight, L — 4–5
- **Presser Foot:** All-purpose foot
- **Needles:** Match to fabric
- **Threads:** Needle — All-purpose polyester or cotton
  Bobbin — All-purpose polyester or silk
- **Tension:** Loosened needle

FABRIC CHOICES:

Woven and knit fabrics

ADDITIONAL SUPPLIES:

- Air- or water-soluble fabric marker

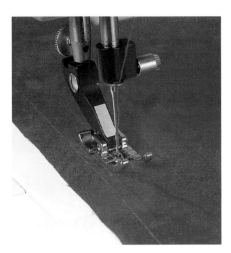

1 Mark the seamline with a fabric marker before beginning to sew. Stitch ¼" on each side of the seamline, leaving 4"–6" of thread at each end.

2 Anchor the threads at one end with a pin and pull the bobbin threads from the other, adjusting the gathers evenly as desired.

3 Change the stitch length to a normal setting. Pin and stitch the gathered fabric to a flat piece, such as a waistband, sewing on the seamline between the two rows of gathering stitches. After stitching, remove the lower row of gathering stitches.

4 Press the seam allowance into the waistband. (Note: When pressing the gathers, point the tip of the iron into the gathers, rather than moving it across them. This will preserve the softness of the gathers and avoid pressing creases into them.) Topstitch from the right side, next to the fold.

Tip Use a contrasting color of thread in the needle to make it easier to see when pulling and removing the gathering threads.

When gathering a full width of fabric, pull threads until half of fabric width is gathered. Anchor threads and pull from other end to finish gathering.

GATHERING, CLEAR ELASTIC

Using a narrow strip of clear elastic to gather fabric makes it easy to match the gathered piece to the flat one. This is an excellent method for projects such as jumpers made of light- to mediumweight fabrics. It will also work with some heavier fabrics such as corduroy or denim; however the lightweight elastic may not be sturdy enough to gather very heavy fabrics.

After sewing the gathered fabric to a flat piece, there is no need to remove the elastic; it is lightweight and thin, adding no discernible bulk to the seam.

MACHINE SET-UP

♦ **Stitch:** Running or sewn-out zig zag stitch, L — 3–5, W — slightly narrower than the elastic
♦ **Presser Foot:** All-purpose foot
♦ **Needles:** Match to fabric
♦ **Threads:** Needle and bobbin — All-purpose polyester or cotton
♦ **Tension:** Normal

FABRIC CHOICES:

Woven and knit fabrics

ADDITIONAL SUPPLIES:

♦ Narrow, clear elastic
♦ Chalk or fabric marker

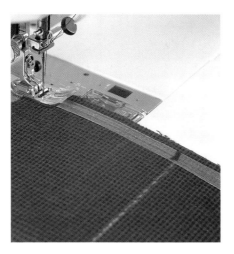

1 Cut a length of elastic the same size as the edge to which the gathers will be sewn. With a fabric marker, draw lines to divide the elastic into quarters. Using a fabric marker or chalk, fold and mark the edge to be gathered in quarters.

2 Place the elastic about ¼" away from the edge of the fabric to be gathered. Stitch a few stitches, anchoring the elastic. Begin stretching the elastic while stitching it to the fabric, matching all the marks.

3 Sew the gathered edge to the appropriate flat edge and construct the project as usual.

Tip Draw the quarter lines 4"– 6" long on the fabric to be gathered to make them easier to see while you are stitching.

GATHERING, OVER CORD

Excellent for gathering heavier fabrics such as corduroy or drapery fabric, a heavy-duty cord is used to pull the fabric along forming the gathers. Use a foot with space on the sole, such as an embroidery or cording foot, to guide the cord and not inhibit the feeding.

MACHINE SET-UP

◆ **Stitch:** Zig zag, L — 2–4, W — 1–3
◆ **Presser Foot:** Cording or embroidery foot
◆ **Needles:** Match to fabric
◆ **Threads:** Needle and bobbin — All-purpose polyester or cotton
   Filler — Gimp cord, Perle Cotton, or dental floss

FABRIC CHOICES:

As desired

1 Position the cord in the seam allowance and place the fabric under the foot. Stitch over the cord without stitching into it, leaving 4"– 6" of cord at each end.

2 Trim the threads, but **not the cord**, from each end. If one end was **not** anchored with the stitching, tie a knot for this purpose. Pull the cord from the opposite end and adjust the gathers evenly.

HEM FINISHES, CORDED

Create a strong and durable hemmed edge especially suited for table linens, garment hems, and home decorating projects. This easy, two-step technique is accomplished quickly with professional results.

MACHINE SET-UP

- ♦ **Stitch:** Zig zag, Step One: L — ½–¾, W — 1–1½; Step Two: L — ½, W — 2–3
- ♦ **Presser Foot:** Cording foot, open embroidery foot
- ♦ **Needles:** Match to fabric
- ♦ **Threads:** Needle — All-purpose polyester, cotton or rayon embroidery
  Bobbin — All-purpose polyester
  Filler — Gimp or topstitching thread
- ♦ **Tension:** Normal
- ♦ **Optional:** Engage needle down function

ADDITIONAL SUPPLIES:

- ♦ Air- or water-soluble fabric or chalk marker
- ♦ Appliqué or fine, embroidery scissors
- ♦ Seam sealant

FABRIC CHOICES:

Woven fabrics only

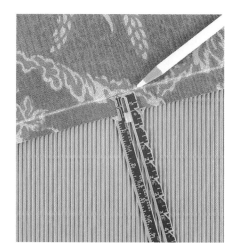

1 Draw a line approximately ½" up from the cut fabric edge. This is where the hem will be sewn.

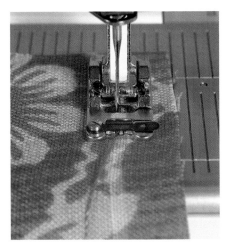

2 Attach the cording foot to the machine, threading filler cord or gimp through the hole. Set the machine for the Step One.

Position the center of the foot on the drawn line. Zig-zag following the line, allowing the stitches to sew over the cord. Clip the excess cord tail.

3 Carefully trim away the seam allowance close to the stitching.

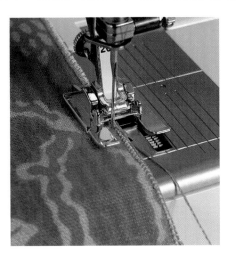

4 Change the machine to the second setting. Attach the open embroidery foot. Sew over the first row of stitching with the left swing of the needle entering the fabric and the right swing falling off the edge. You will be creating a raised, satin stitch edge. Clip the thread tails and dot the ends with seam sealant.

5 If a heavier corded edge is desired, lay a second strand of filler cord next to the first couched strand. Cover both filler cords when sewing the second set of zig zag stitches.

HEM FINISHES, DECORATIVE STITCH

Explore your machine's decorative possibilities by sewing your next hem using a combination of decorative stitches. Create a band of color and design interest by sewing combinations of motifs and words. Select subtle tone-on-tone embroidery for elegant effects or choose colorful contrasts for children's wear. Don't overlook the architectural appeal of utility stitches, too!

MACHINE SET-UP

- ◆ **Stitch:** Decorative stitches in any combination, L and W — adjust as needed
- ◆ **Presser Foot:** Open or clear embroidery foot
- ◆ **Needles:** Match to fabric
- ◆ **Tension:** Slightly loosened needle
- ◆ **Optional:** Mirror image, single pattern and memory functions all for design capabilities

FABRIC CHOICES:

Woven and knit fabrics

ADDITIONAL SUPPLIES:

- ◆ Air- or water-soluble fabric marker
- ◆ Clear ruler
- ◆ Tear-away stabilizer for thread-heavy designs on woven fabrics; liquid or spray-on fabric stabilizers on crosswise knits

1 Turn up and press a hem allowance. Mark the lines to be sewn using the fabric marker and clear ruler. For woven fabrics, place a layer of tear-away stabilizer underneath. If using a knit, paint a layer of liquid stabilizer, or spray the area to be stitched with multiple sprays of spray-on fabric stabilizer. (Note: Either product will stabilize the natural stretch in the knit and avoid crosswise stretching.) Or, fuse a temporary stabilizer developed just for knits. On some knits, an extra layer of tear-away stabilizer may be needed.

2 Following the marked line, sew in the first row, stitching though both hem layers.

3 Continue to sew multiple decorative rows until the desired hem band is complete. Remove the tear-away stabilizer or any liquid or spray-on product according to manufacturer's directions.

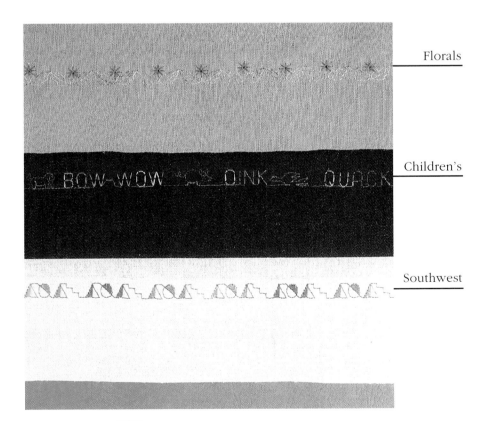

Florals

Children's

Southwest

HEM FINISHES, DOUBLE AND TRIPLE NEEDLE

Decoratively finish your hem edges with multi-colored, perfect, parallel rows of stitching using double and triple needles. Two or three needles of equal size are mounted onto one needle bar, allowing the sewer to sew multiple rows with only one stitching. Highlight plain fabric hems by using different color threads in each needle and either a straight or narrow zig zag stitch. As an added bonus, the raw edges from the hem allowance are covered by the zig zag stitch created by the bobbin thread connecting all the needle threads!

MACHINE SET-UP

- **Stitch:** Straight or narrow zig zag stitches, W — select carefully
- **Presser Foot:** Open or clear embroidery foot
- **Needles:** Double needle, size #1.6 to #8.0 widths available. Check your machine manual for sizes recommended for triple needles
- **Threads:** Needle — All-purpose polyester or cotton or rayon embroidery
  Bobbin — All-purpose polyester
- **Tension:** Normal
- **Optional:** Engage the double needle limitation

FABRIC CHOICES:

Woven fabrics and stabilized knits

ADDITIONAL SUPPLIES:

- Air- or water-soluble fabric marker
- Clear ruler

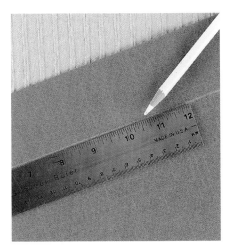

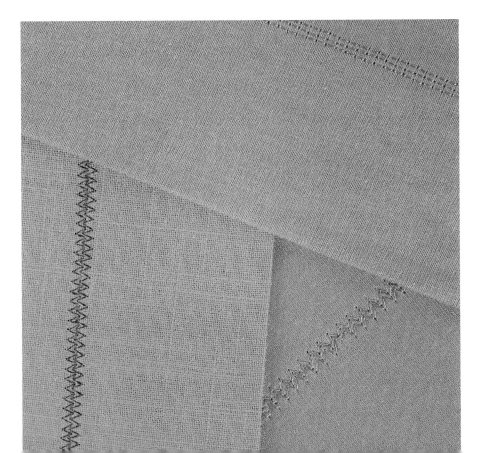

1 Turn up and press in the desired hem allowance. Install a double or triple needle. Refer to your sewing machine manual for the recommended thread path for each thread. If desired, draw in the top of the pressed hem allowance to act as a guide for sewing.

Tip Let your sewing machine be your best guide on stitch width. The opening in the throat plate, divided by the distance between the left and right needle gives you the approximate stitch width that can be used.

2 From the right side, center the needles on top of the drawn line at the top of the hem allowance. Begin to sew at a medium speed, allowing the needles to form the stitch correctly with the single bobbin thread.

3 For a double needle shadow hem, thread the needles and bobbin thread with a darker color. Sew in the hem, creating a shadow effect on fine, lightweight fabrics.

HEM FINISHES, HEMMER FEET

Hemmer feet add a new dimension to your sewing repertoire by making hem or edge finishing easy. Each foot has a groove on the bottom to accommodate the roll of the different weights of fabric while stitching. The wider the groove, the heavier the fabric the foot will accommodate. Certain hemmer feet are designed to make shell hemming much easier. Check with your sewing machine dealer for help in purchasing the correct foot for your project.

MACHINE SET-UP

- ♦ **Stitch:** Straight, L — 2–2½; zig zag, all-forward stretch, or blindhem for shell hemming
- ♦ **Presser Foot:** 2mm, 3mm, 4mm, 5mm, 6mm hemmer feet
- ♦ **Needles:** Match to fabric
- ♦ **Threads:** Needle and bobbin — All-purpose polyester
- ♦ **Tension:** Normal
- ♦ **Optional:** Engage needle down function

FABRIC CHOICES:

As a general rule, firmly woven lighter weight fabrics work best. Bulky or stretchy fabrics are not appropriate. Tricot or single knits for shell hemming.

ADDITIONAL SUPPLIES:

- ♦ Light- to medium weight tear-away stabilizer or adding machine paper
- ♦ Edging lace

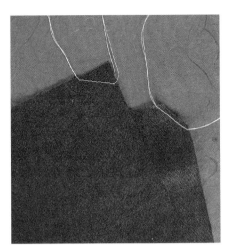

1 To start a rolled hem, take a few stitches across the corner of your fabric. Trim the fabric away close to the stitching, leaving the long thread tails.

2 Select the correct hemmer foot for the weight of your fabric. Holding the thread tails, gently pull the end of the fabric into the scroll of the hemmer foot. Lower the needle into the folded edge and lower the foot.

3 Begin sewing slowly, holding the edge of the fabric between the thumb and index finger of your right hand. Keep your hand stable, letting the fabric slide through your fingers.

4 Larger hemmers will handle heavier fabrics. Some hemmer attachments actually fit on the needle plate in front of the all-purpose foot.

continued

5 A shell hem is achieved on fine, lightweight fabrics using a zig zag, all-forward stretch, or blindhem stitch. Stabilize the edge of the fabric with tear-away stabilizer or paper before sewing. Stitch the hem as usual.

6 Sew lace into the rolled hem as an added embellishment. First, baste the lace ⅜" from the edge. Roll the hem in the same manner as described on the previous page, covering the straight edge of the lace.

7 Press the rolled hem back away from the lace. All raw edges are encased within the hem.

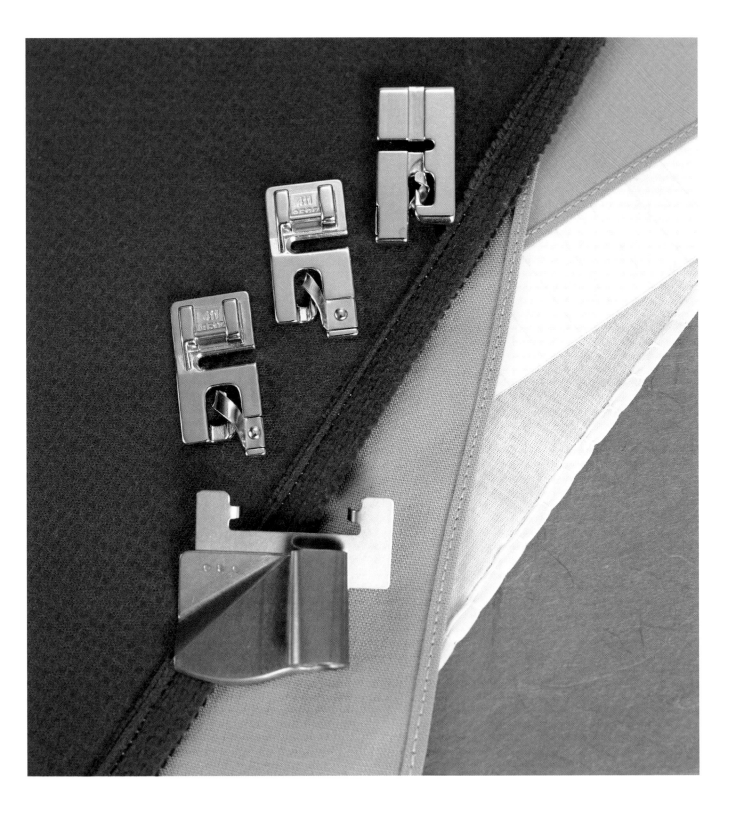

HEM FINISHES, HEMSTITCHED

Consider finishing your next garment's sleeve or skirt hem with the classic look of hemstitching. Adaptable to many stitch patterns, this hem finish is sewn with a wing needle on either a single or double folded hem. This hem finish is perfect for sheer fabrics and is a classic choice for elegant table and bed linens.

MACHINE SET-UP

Single Fold Hems
♦ **Stitch:** Daisy/star stitch, L and W — $2\frac{1}{2}$; or programmed entredeux, L — $2\frac{1}{2}$, W — 3

Double Fold Hems
♦ **Stitch:** Pin or blanket stitch, L — $2\frac{1}{2}$–3, W — 3
♦ **Presser Foot:** Open or clear embroidery foot
♦ **Needles:** Single Wing needle, size #100
♦ **Threads:** Needle — Cotton or rayon embroidery
  Bobbin — 60 wt. cotton embroidery or all-purpose polyester
♦ **Tension:** Normal
♦ **Optional:** Engage needle down function

FABRIC CHOICES:

Natural fibers, such as all-cotton organdy, organza, linen, and batiste

ADDITIONAL SUPPLIES:

♦ Appliqué or sharp embroidery scissors
♦ Spray starch

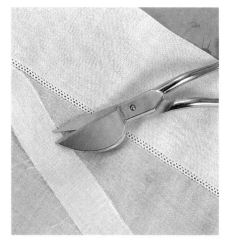

1 Spray-starch the area to be hemmed; press dry. Cut the bottom edge of the garment as evenly as possible. Fold up the desired hem depth as follows. For single fold hems, fold up the hem allowance plus 1". For double fold hems, fold up ½" at the lower edge then fold up the remaining hem.

2 On the right side, place your presser foot and needle so the stitching will be 1" down from the top raw edge of the pressed up single fold hem allowance. Select the desired stitch and sew at an even speed. Your stitching will sew entirely onto the hem allowance.

3 Trim away the excess hem allowance close to the top of the stitching from the wrong side.

4 For double fold hems, from the wrong side, position the presser foot and needle so that the vertical part of the stitch is right next to the double-folded edge and the horizontal stitch sews onto the hem allowance.

HEM FINISHES, RAISED DOUBLE NEEDLE

Replicate the look of corded piping without the cord by sewing on a single layer of fabric using a double needle and increased tension. This technique is especially fun on knits, duplicating ready-to-wear hems.

MACHINE SET-UP

- ♦ **Stitch:** Straight or running stitch, L and W — Preset
- ♦ **Presser Foot:** Open or clear embroidery foot or all-purpose foot
- ♦ **Needles:** Double needle, size #1.6/70 – 8.0/80 for straight stitching; #1.6/70 – 3.0/80 for running stitch
- ♦ **Threads:** Needle — All-purpose polyester, cotton or rayon embroidery
  Bobbin — All-purpose polyester
- ♦ **Tension:** Slightly tightened needle, at least 2 steps above normal setting. Increase if needed for heavier fabrics
- ♦ **Optional:** Engage double needle limitation

FABRIC CHOICES:

Lightweight woven and knit fabrics

ADDITIONAL SUPPLIES:

- ♦ Air- or water-soluble fabric marker
- ♦ Clear ruler

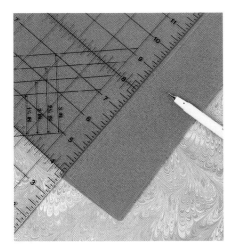

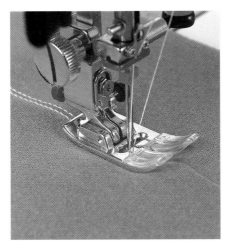

1 If desired, draw in a stitching guideline using a fabric marking tool and clear ruler. Follow Step 1 found in "Hem Finishes, Double and Triple Needles".

2 Center and position the needles over the pressed hem. Begin to sew the hem. The stitching will create a raised texture and sew the hem allowance in one operation. Draw needle threads to the wrong side and knot with the bobbin threads.

3 This technique is especially effective when sewn in multiple rows for a hem.

Tip Be sure to test the size of the double needle and the stitch you have chosen. Some needles may be spaced too far apart for the preset width of your chosen stitch. Use a smaller spaced needle rather than narrowing the width of the stitch.

HEM FINISHES, SHADOW

Most often seen on children's heirloom clothing, this hemming technique features a colored fabric insert placed within a folded hem for a gentle touch of color. Continue the color story by stitching the hem using coordinating thread as an accent color. This hem is especially effective when sewn with a scalloped upper hem edge.

MACHINE SET-UP

♦ **Stitch:** Pin stitch, L — 1½, W — 2½
♦ **Presser Foot:** Open or clear embroidery or appliqué foot or edgestitch foot
♦ **Needles:** Single wing needle, size #100
♦ **Threads:** Needle — Cotton or rayon embroidery
  Bobbin — All-purpose polyester
♦ **Tension:** Normal
♦ **Optional:** Engage mirror image if necessary

FABRIC CHOICES:

Sheer, all natural fibers, such as cotton, organdy, or batiste

ADDITIONAL SUPPLIES:

♦ Air- or water-soluble fabric or chalk marker
♦ Appliqué or sharp embroidery scissors
♦ Spray starch

 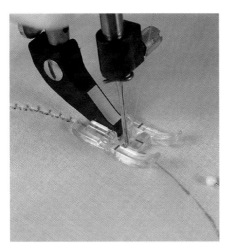 

1 Spray-starch the entire hem allowance and lower garment edge. Fold up the desired hem allowance. The hem depth should be between 4"–6" deep. Using a curved edge and a marker, draw in a scallop-shaped hemline to use as a guide for sewing. Insert a band of contrasting colored fabric between the folded hem layers. Pin all three layers together.

2 From the right side, position the center of the appliqué foot or the blade of the edgestitch foot along the drawn line. The stright stitch portion of the stitch should fall parallel to the drawn scallop line, and the horizontal part of the stitch should sew inside the hem allowance. Sew all three layers together.

3 When the hem is finished, from the wrong side, carefully trim away the excess hem fabric above the stitching. Spray-starch and press the finished hem.

MITERING CORNERS

At some point in every sewer's career a project will arise that calls for perfectly sewn corners. Mitered corners eliminate bulk at lower pocket edges and at open side hems. Follow these simple steps for easy miters and add a couture touch to your next garment.

MACHINE SET-UP

♦ **Stitch:** Straight, L — 2–2½
♦ **Presser Foot:** All-purpose foot
♦ **Needles:** Match to fabric
♦ **Threads:** Needle and bobbin — All-purpose polyester
♦ **Tension:** Normal

FABRIC CHOICES:

Appropriate to most fabrics

ADDITIONAL SUPPLIES:

♦ Fusible web for No-Sew Method
♦ Chalk or fabric marker

No-Sew Method

1 Draw in a hem allowance on the hem edge.

2 Iron a crease along the drawn lines. Open the fabric flat.

3 Fold the lower pocket corners on the diagonal to form a triangle. The intersecting side creases will be at the middle of the fold of the triangle. Press.

4 Trim the pressed triangle to a ⅜" seam allowance.

5 Open up the triangle and press in the corners diagonally along the crease lines. Insert a small piece of fusible web into the cor-

ners; press. (Note: You will have perfectly fused, square corners to stitch into your garment.)

Sew Method

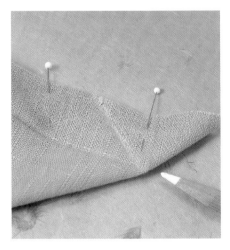

1 Follow Steps 1 through 3 above to mark and crease the fabric. Fold the fabric at the corners matching the raw edges to form a triangle. Draw a line at a right angle to the fold, intersecting the crease marks.

2 Sew along the marked lines.

3 Trim the seam, turn right sides out, and press.

SEAM FINISHES, EDGE-STITCHED

Traditional fine sewing techniques teach that the inside of a garment must be as beautiful as the outside. There are a multitude of fine seam finishes available for most every fabric created. The Seam Finishes section lists a few of the most traditional techniques.

Perfect for soft, pliable fabrics, this edge-stitched seam finish is weightless and almost invisible, ideal for sheers and lightweight woven fabrics.

MACHINE SET-UP

- **Stitch:** Zig zag, L — 1½–2, W approximately ¾–1
- **Presser Foot:** Edgestitch foot
- **Needles:** Match to fabric
- **Threads:** Needle and bobbin — 60 wt. cotton embroidery
- **Tension:** Normal
- **Optional:** Adjust needle position

FABRIC CHOICES:

Light- to medium weight wovens and sheers

1 With this technique, it is easier to finish the seam allowances prior to constructing the garment. Taking the pressed and stitched clean-finished edge into consideration, adjust the width of your seam allowance in order not to alter the garment fit.

2 Press under at least a ¼" along the edge of the seam allowance.

3 Place the fabric, right side up, underneath the edgestitch foot. Position the foot so the blade or edge of the toe rests against the pressed fold. Adjust the needle position, if necessary, so the left-hand swing of the needle sews into the fold and the right-hand swing falls just off the outer folded edge. Sew the edge, allowing the blade on the foot to act as a guide for perfect sewing.

4 Trim the excess fabric from the wrong side and press.

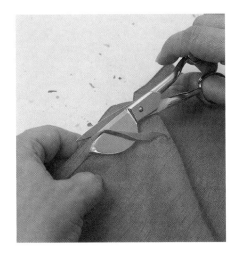

SEAM FINISHES,
FLAT FELLED

Flat felled seams are most often found on sports-

wear or casual or reversible garments usually

constructed from woven fabrics. Characterized

by a clean-finished, double-sewn seam, this two-

step technique first joins the garment sections,

then clean-finishes the seam with a folded and

topstitched edge. Take advantage of simplifying

this seemingly tricky seam by using a flat fell or

lap seam presser foot available from most sewing

machine manufacturers. These feet are designed

to accurately gauge fabric feed and stitching.

MACHINE SET-UP

- ♦ **Stitch:** Straight, L — 2½–3 depending on fabric weight
- ♦ **Presser Foot:** Flat fell or lap seam foot
- ♦ **Needles:** Universal or denim needle, size #90
- ♦ **Threads:** Needle and bobbin — All-purpose polyester
- ♦ **Tension:** Normal
- ♦ **Optional:** Adjust needle position

FABRIC CHOICES:

Medium to heavy weight wovens, from shirting to heavy denim and upholstery

1 Pin the fabrics, wrong sides together, extending the bottom piece ¼"–½" beyond the edge of the upper layer.

2 Fold the lower fabric over the top fabric layer, keeping the folded edge even with the right edge of the presser foot. Adjust the

needle position to sew near the raw edge of the folded fabric. Sew three to four stitches to secure.

3 Lower the needle, lift the foot and guide the fabric over the slot on the toe. The raw edge should not extend past the inside of the left toe. Sew the seam. Press the seam flat, then to the left.

4 Place the pressed seam between the two toes of the presser foot, with the fold facing the left side. Adjust the needle position so that the needle stitches close to the folded edge.

5 Stitch the encased seam allowance in place. Press flat.

Tip Heavier, topstitching thread may be used for the final stitching in Steps 4 and 5 if a more decorative look is desired.

SEAM FINISHES, FRENCH

Encase the seams in sheer and silky fabrics in the classic manner with French seams. This double-sewn seam is first sewn wrong sides together, then right sides together. The seam finish looks delicate, but actually is quite strong.

MACHINE SET-UP

- ♦ **Stitch:** Straight, L — 2–3 depending upon fabric
- ♦ **Presser Foot:** All-purpose foot, edgestitch, or ¼" foot
- ♦ **Needles:** Match to fabric
- ♦ **Threads:** Needle and bobbin — All-purpose polyester or silk thread for extra fine fabrics
- ♦ **Tension:** Normal
- ♦ **Optional:** Adjust needle position

FABRIC CHOICES:

Lightweight sheer or silky woven fabrics

ADDITIONAL SUPPLIES:

- ♦ Rotary cutter and mat or sharp scissors
- ♦ Clear ruler
- ♦ Spray starch for extremely light weight fabrics

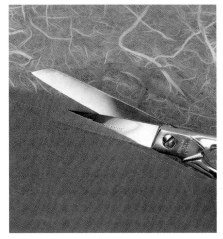

1 Spray-starch the seam allowances, if necessary, on very soft or silky fabric. Pin the seam allowances, wrong sides together.

2 Using the all-purpose presser foot and an adjusted needle position, sew a ⅜" wide seam from the raw edge.

3 Using a rotary cutter and ruler or very sharp scissors, trim the seam allowance to ⅛". Open the seam and press the seam allowance to the backside of the garment.

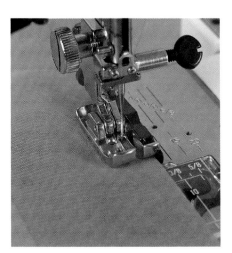

4 Pin the garment right sides together, encasing the trimmed, previously sewn seam. Using the edgestitch or ¼" foot, place the blade along the sewn seam. Adjust the needle to sew a ¼" seam, encasing the raw edges. Sew the seam and press.

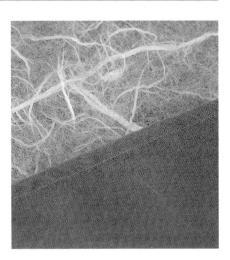

SEAM FINISHES, HONG KONG

Beautifully wrapped seam edges, called a Hong Kong seam finish, are a treat for the eyes in unlined garments. Strips of lightweight bias-cut fabrics encase the raw edges of each individual seam for a couture look. Recycled, cleaned men's neckties are a wonderful source for colorful bias silk, perfect for these bindings!

MACHINE SET-UP

- ♦ **Stitch:** Straight, L — 2½
- ♦ **Presser Foot:** ¼" foot, edgestitch foot
- ♦ **Needles:** Match to fabric
- ♦ **Threads:** Needle and bobbin — All-purpose polyester
- ♦ **Tension:** Normal
- ♦ **Optional:** Adjust needle position

FABRIC CHOICES:

Lightweight bias-cut cottons, batiste, or cleaned silk ties

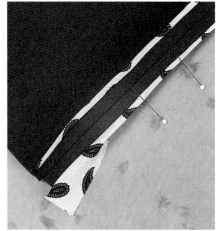

1 Cut 1" bias strips for seam edges. Refer to page 268, "Bias Binding", for an easy method for creating yards of continuous bias strips. Attach the ¼" foot on the sewing machine.

2 With right sides together, sew the bias strip to the raw edge of the seam allowance using a ¼" seam. Trim the seam to ⅛". Press the seam allowance flat.

3 Attach the edgestitch foot. Wrap the bias binding to the wrong side of the seam allowance and pin.

4 Place the folded edge of the binding against the blade of the edgestitch foot. Adjust the needle position to sew in the ditch created by the first seam. Trim any excess bias binding from the wrong side.

SEAM FINISHES, TRICOT BOUND

Look for pre-packaged, tricot binding strips to sew quick and easy bound seams. These strips are sewn onto raw edges in one step using a zig zag stitch. The nature of the tricot fabric allows itself to automatically wrap around the seam edge when pulled. Tricot binding strips are sold on a roll in neutral colors and available in ⅝" and 1¼" widths. Select the ⅝" width for binding most seam edges.

MACHINE SET-UP

♦ **Stitch:** Zig zag, L and W — approximately ½–2
♦ **Presser Foot:** Zig zag foot
♦ **Needles:** Match to fabric
♦ **Threads:** Needle and bobbin — All-purpose polyester
♦ **Tension:** Normal
♦ **Optional:** Engage needle down function

FABRIC CHOICES:

Especially good choice for loosely woven fabrics used in unlined garments.

ADDITIONAL SUPPLIES:

♦ ⅝" wide tricot binding

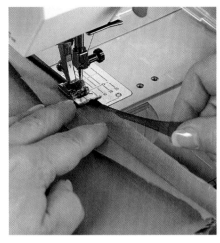

1 Press the sewn ⅝" seam allowances flat.

2 Turn back the garment from the seam edge to be bound, exposing a single layer of the seam allowance. Cut a piece of the tricot binding at least 1" longer than the seam allowance to be bound.

3 Take a few zig zag stitches to position and establish the fold in the tricot strip and secure it in place. With the needle in the fabric, begin to zig zag the binding in place, with the stitches close to the cut edge. Gently tug on the tricot strip to encourage it to wrap around the seam allowance edge. Wrap and stitch all seam edges in this manner.

TOPSTITCHING

Even topstitching on a jacket lapel, pocket, collar, or cuff can be the final professional touch to your garment. A straight stitch and heavier top-stitching thread makes this a very simple technique to sew. Use the proper foot or guide to assure that your stitching is straight.

MACHINE SET-UP

- ♦ **Stitch:** Straight, L — 2–4
- ♦ **Presser Foot:** Edgestitch or all-purpose foot with quilting guide
- ♦ **Needles:** Topstitching needle, size #90–#110
- ♦ **Threads:** Needle — Topstitching
  Bobbin — Topstitching or all-purpose polyester
- ♦ **Tension:** Normal, though test first
- ♦ **Optional:** Engage needle down function

FABRIC CHOICES:

As desired

1 Thread your machine with top-stitching thread. If the area to be topstitched is reversible, wind top-stitching thread on your bobbin, too. Test first and adjust your tension if necessary.

2 Place the finished or folded edge of the fabric under the foot next to the blade. Using the blade as your guide, stitch along the edge pivoting at corners.

3 When the topstitching is completed, pull both needle and bobbin threads to one side and knot. Using a large-eye needle, thread the tails back between the layers of fabric. Trim.

ZIPPERS, CENTERED

A centered zipper is most often the first zipper technique learned by beginning sewers. Two evenly stitched, parallel tucks of fabric meet to cover the centered zipper teeth. Thanks to a few new tips and products, foolproof positioning and perfect topstitching is possible every time.

MACHINE SET-UP

- ♦ **Stitch:** Straight, L — 2½
- ♦ **Presser Foot:** Adjustable zipper foot
- ♦ **Needles:** Match to fabric
- ♦ **Threads:** Needle and bobbin — All-purpose polyester
- ♦ **Tension:** Normal
- ♦ **Optional:** Adjust needle position

FABRIC CHOICES:

As desired

ADDITIONAL SUPPLIES:

- ♦ Zipper, 2″ longer than needed
- ♦ ¼″-wide strips of fusible web

1 On most all zipper techniques, insert the zipper while the garment is as flat as possible. Steam press the zipper flat. Fuse narrow strips of fusible web to each side of the zipper tape, close to the

finished outer edge. With right sides together, baste the seam allowance closed. Remove the paper backing from the fusible web strips.

2 Position the zipper so that the bottom stop is at the end of the basted seam. The zipper will extend past the top of the garment to allow for easy and straight topstitching.

3 From the right side, adjust the needle position to the right so that the needle sews approximately ¼" away from the basted center seamline. Stitch one side of the zipper from top to bottom.

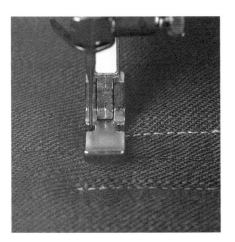

4 Beginning at the top edge, sew the opposite side of the zipper, adjusting the needle position to the left. Sew in the zipper from top to bottom, pivoting at the lower edge to sew horizontally across the bottom of the zipper. If your zipper foot has an

adjustable guide, slide the guide so it rides along the seamline to assure straight stitching. (Note: This directional method of sewing is applicable to all zipper applications and keeps the fabric from twisting when the sides of thezipper are sewn in opposite directions.)

5 Remove the basting stitches. Pull the zipper tab below the garment top edge. Clip the excess zipper tape and bartack across each side of the zipper teeth to assure that the pull remains on the zipper when the garment is being worn.

ZIPPERS, HAND-PICKED

Display the elegance of a handpicked zipper in your next garment, stitched in half the time using the sewing machine. A simple two-step process inserts the zipper with a straight stitch, then finishes with a blindhem stitch for a beautiful couture touch.

MACHINE SET-UP

- ♦ **Stitch:** Straight, L — 2½; blindhem, L — 2½–3
- ♦ **Presser Foot:** Zipper foot, blindhem foot
- ♦ **Needles:** Match to fabric
- ♦ **Threads:** Needle and bobbin — All-purpose polyester
- ♦ **Tension:** Normal
- ♦ **Optional:** Adjust needle position

FABRIC CHOICES:

As desired

ADDITIONAL SUPPLIES:

- ♦ Zipper, 2" longer than needed

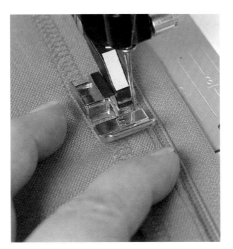

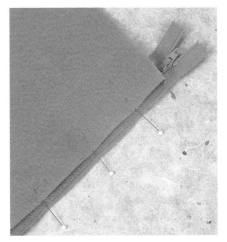

1 Place the closed zipper, right side down, on the right seam allowance. The coils should be right next to, but not on, the seam. Sew the zipper tape to the seam allowance only, adjusting the needle position.

2 Fold the zipper back on the stitching. Adjust the needle position to the right and sew ⅛" away from the folded edge of the fabric through both layers of fabric and the zipper tape.

3 From the right side, fold back the unstitched side so the seam allowance and the zipper tape are now exposed.

4 Position the guide on the blindhem foot so that blade rests along the fold.

5 Sew into the zipper tape and seam allowance, just barely catching the garment face along the fold with the zig zag portion of the stitch. Press the zipper placket

when stitching is complete. Tiny horizontal stitches will appear on the left side of the seamline, replicating hand stitching. Follow the last step of "Zippers, Centered".

ZIPPERS, INVISIBLE

Discreetly tucked into the seamline, invisible zippers lend a designer touch to any garment. Seeming to float in a garment with no visible stitching, this zipper technique is the least obtrusive and most elegant of all zipper applications. Special invisible zipper feet with multi-grooved soles are available; however, a wide variety of other feet can be chosen.

MACHINE SET-UP

- ♦ **Stitch:** Straight, L — 2–2½
- ♦ **Presser Foot:** Zipper foot, buttonhole foot, 3 groove pintuck foot (Any presser foot that has grooves cut into the underside of the foot.)
- ♦ **Needles:** Match to fabric
- ♦ **Threads:** Needle and bobbin — All-purpose polyester
- ♦ **Tension:** Normal
- ♦ **Optional:** Adjust needle position

FABRIC CHOICES:

As desired

ADDITIONAL SUPPLIES:

- ♦ Invisible zipper, same size as opening

1 Lightly crease-mark with an iron the ⅝" seamline to serve as a guide for zipper placement and stitching. (Note: The garment seam is not basted closed prior to installing this type of zipper.)

2 With right sides together, pin the zipper tape to the right side of the garment so that the coil is on the ⅝" cease-marked seamline. Position the coil in the groove on the bottom of your chosen presser foot. Adjust the needle position to sew very close to the coils. Stitch the right side of the zipper.

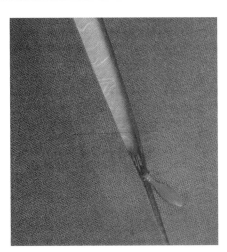

3 Again with right sides together, pin or baste the left zipper to the left side of the garment, placing the coils on the ⅝" seamline. Place the zipper coil in the left groove of the presser foot. Adjust the needle position to sew closely to the coils. Sew in the left side.

4 Switch to the zipper foot and close the zipper. With the garment right sides together, sew the seam starting ½" above the bottom of the zipper. Attach the all-purpose presser foot to complete sewing the balance of the seam.

ZIPPERS, PLACKET

Placket or lapped seam zippers are often used as the side-seam closure of choice rather than a center application. The zipper is offset in the seam allowance creating a larger fold of fabric covering the zipper teeth on the left side. This makes an inconspicuous closing.

MACHINE SET-UP

- ♦ **Stitch:** Straight, L — 2½
- ♦ **Presser Foot:** Zipper foot or zipper foot with adjustable guide
- ♦ **Needles:** Match to fabric
- ♦ **Threads:** Needle and bobbin — All-purpose polyester
- ♦ **Tension:** Normal
- ♦ **Optional:** Adjust needle position

FABRIC CHOICES:

As desired

ADDITIONAL SUPPLIES:

- ♦ Zipper, 2" longer than needed

1 Follow Steps 1 through 3 for "Zipper, Handpicked". Flatten the garment and seam allowances.

2 From the garment right side, adjust the needle position to sew ⅜" away from the basted seamline onto the garment upper layer, seam allowance, and zipper tape. Sew from the top to the bottom, pivoting at the lower edge to sew across the bottom of the zipper.

3 Finish the zipper as described in the final step of "Zipper, Centered ".

IMPORTANT
INFORMATION

For information on the latest machine models and/or to locate an authorized dealer nearest you, contact the following:

Allyn International
Necchi Sewing Machines
1075 Santa Fe Dr.
Denver, CO 80204
1-800-825-9987

Baby Lock USA
1716 Gilsinn Ln.
Fenton, MO 63026
1-800-422-2952
www.babylock.com

Bernina of America
3500 Thayer Ct.
Aurora, IL 60504-6182
1-800-405-2SEW
www.berninausa.com

Brother International
100 Sommerset Corporate Blvd.
Bridgewater, NY 08807
1-800-4-A-BROTHER
www.brother.com

Elna USA
1760 Gilsinn Ln.
Fenton, MO 63026
1-800-848-ELNA
www.elnausa.com

Janome/New Home
10 Industrial Ave.
Mahwah, NJ 07430
1-800-631-0183
www.janome.com

Pfaff American Sales Corporation
610 Winters Ave.
Paramus, NJ 07653
1-800-99-PFAFF
www.pfaff-us-cda.com

Riccar of America
1760 Gilsinn Ln.
Fenton, MO 63026
1-314-349-3000

Sears/Kenmore
JAMAC, Inc.
1822 Brummel Dr.
Elk Grove, IL 60007
1-847-593-1261

Singer
4500 Singer Rd.
Murfreesboro, TN 37130
1-800-474-6437
www.singersewing.com

Viking Sewing Machines Inc.
3100 Viking Pkwy
Westlake, OH 44145
1-800-358-0001
 www.husqvarnaviking.com

White Machine Company
31000 Viking Pkwy
Westlake, OH 44145
1-216-252-3311
www.whitesewing.com

Home Sewing Association
1350 Broadway
New York, NY 10018
www.sewing.org

American Sewing Guild
Association Headquarters
9140 Ward Pkwy.
Kansas City, MO 64114
1-816-444-3500
Fax 1-816-444-0300

ACKNOWLEDGMENTS

The following experienced sewers and writers graciously contributed samples, helped sew techniques, or shared their sewing expertise with us. We truly appreciate their contributions in making this book better.

Susan Beck, Jill Dankelfsen, Louise Dergantz, Sarah Hochhauser, Karen Kunkel, Felicia Smigiel, and Delinda Weiss.

The following samples were generously offered for photography from Louise Baird:

The following samples were seen on the PBS television show, Martha's Sewing Room, Martha Pullen Co.:

The following projects were used at the Martha Pullen School of Art Fashion:

INDEX

INDEX

INDEX

INDEX

INDEX